AUSTRALIA

Contents

New South Wales	6
Australian Capital Territory	94
Victoria	104
Queensland	148
Western Australia	185
Tasmania	206
South Australia	224
Northern Territory	234

The pubs, markets and restaurants of Sydney's historical Rocks district attract tourists and locals alike

The Sydney Harbour Bridge at dusk never fails to impress. Next page: Bondi Beach is an Australian icon

10 Luna Park for family fun

Late night patrons flock to Harry's Cafe de Wheels

Darling Harbour's dining and shopping hub is abuzz with activity day and night. Next page: popular Manly beach

Sydney's early settlers made The Rocks district their home and its character-filled streets have been preserved

16　The Strand shopping arcade has been selling fine wares for generations

Sydney's ornate Queen Victoria Building was built as a produce market in the 19th century

Harbourside parks offer stunning views of the city centre and Harbour Bridge

The city is punctuated by Sydney Tower which offers visitors panoramic views from the top

The Opera House is a World Heritage-listed site and is one of the most distinctive 20th century buildings in the world

An array of multi-coloured lights bring Sydney's skyline to life as day turns into night

Traffic speeds along Sydney's Harbour Bridge when the work day ends and it's time to head home

24 A bird's-eye view of Sydney

Next page: Observatory Hill is a vantage point for views north over the Harbour

28 · The Harbour Bridge provides a magnificent backdrop to a foreshore stroll

The grand finale on New Year's Eve is a spray of light off the Harbour Bridge. Next page: a sun-bathed day in Double Bay

34 Boats race on Sydney Harbour

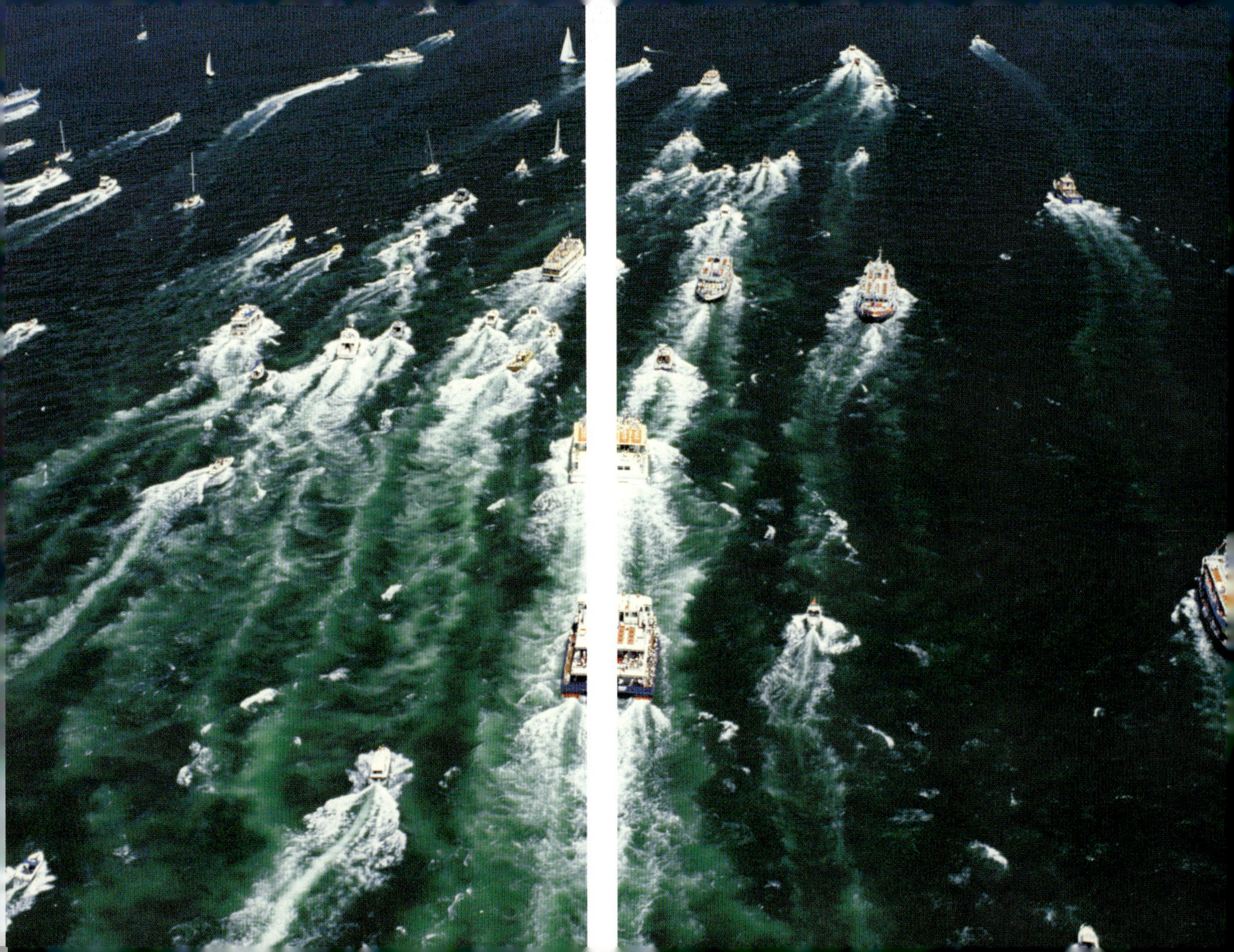

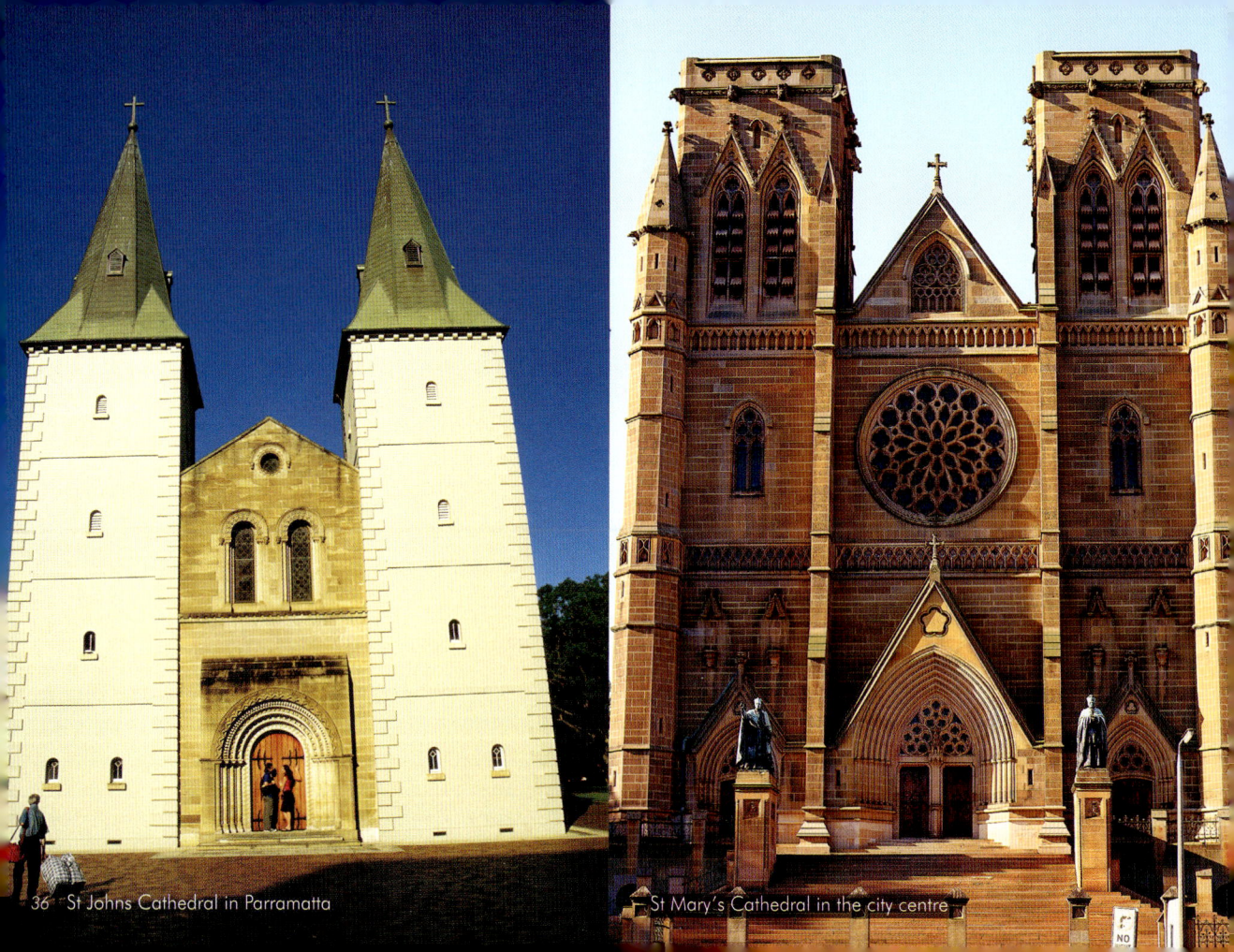

36 St Johns Cathedral in Parramatta St Mary's Cathedral in the city centre

The grand entry to the State Library of New South Wales | 37

Doyle's seafood restaurant at Watson's Bay

Outdoor eating and drinking is a way of life.
Next page: The Spit in Sydney's north

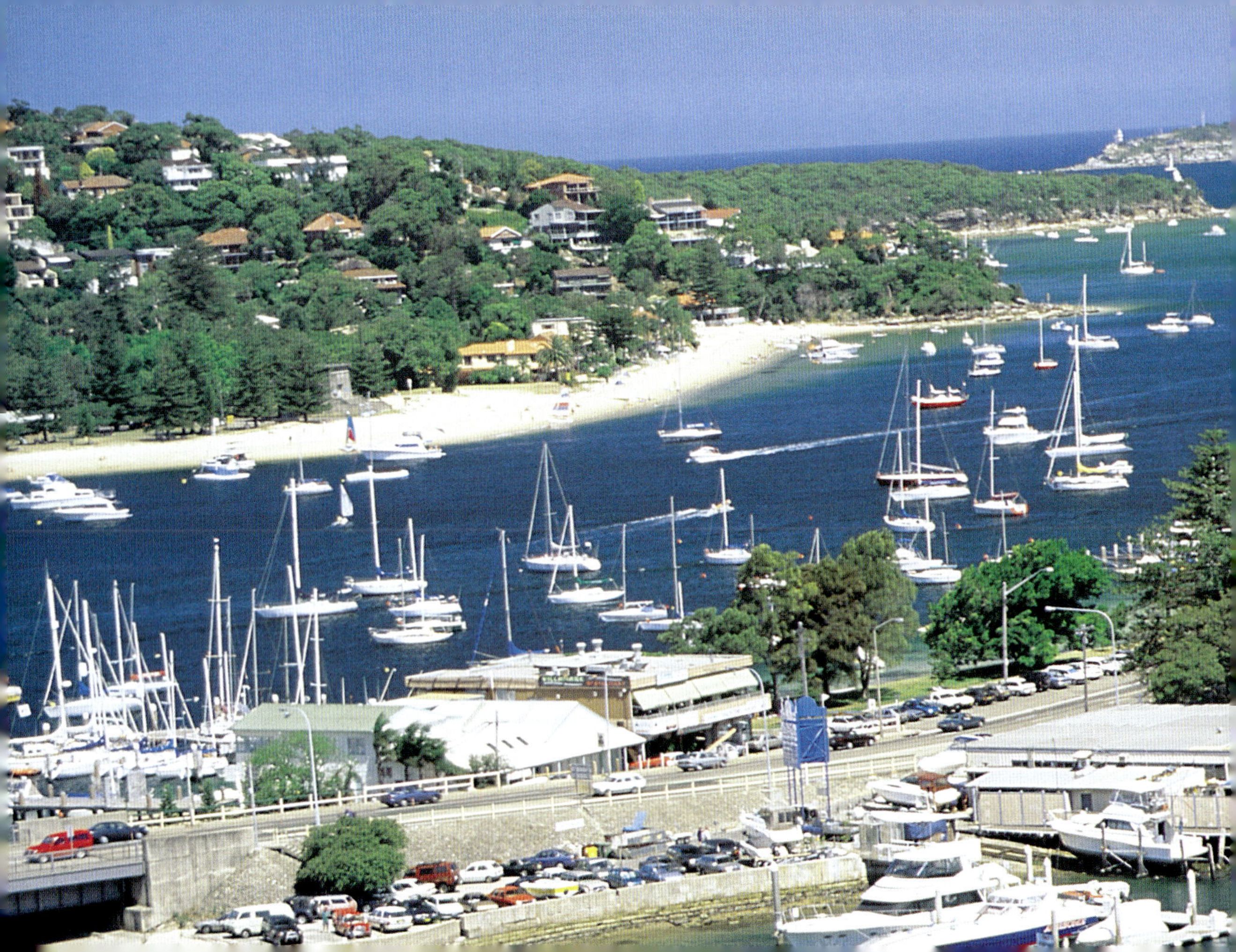

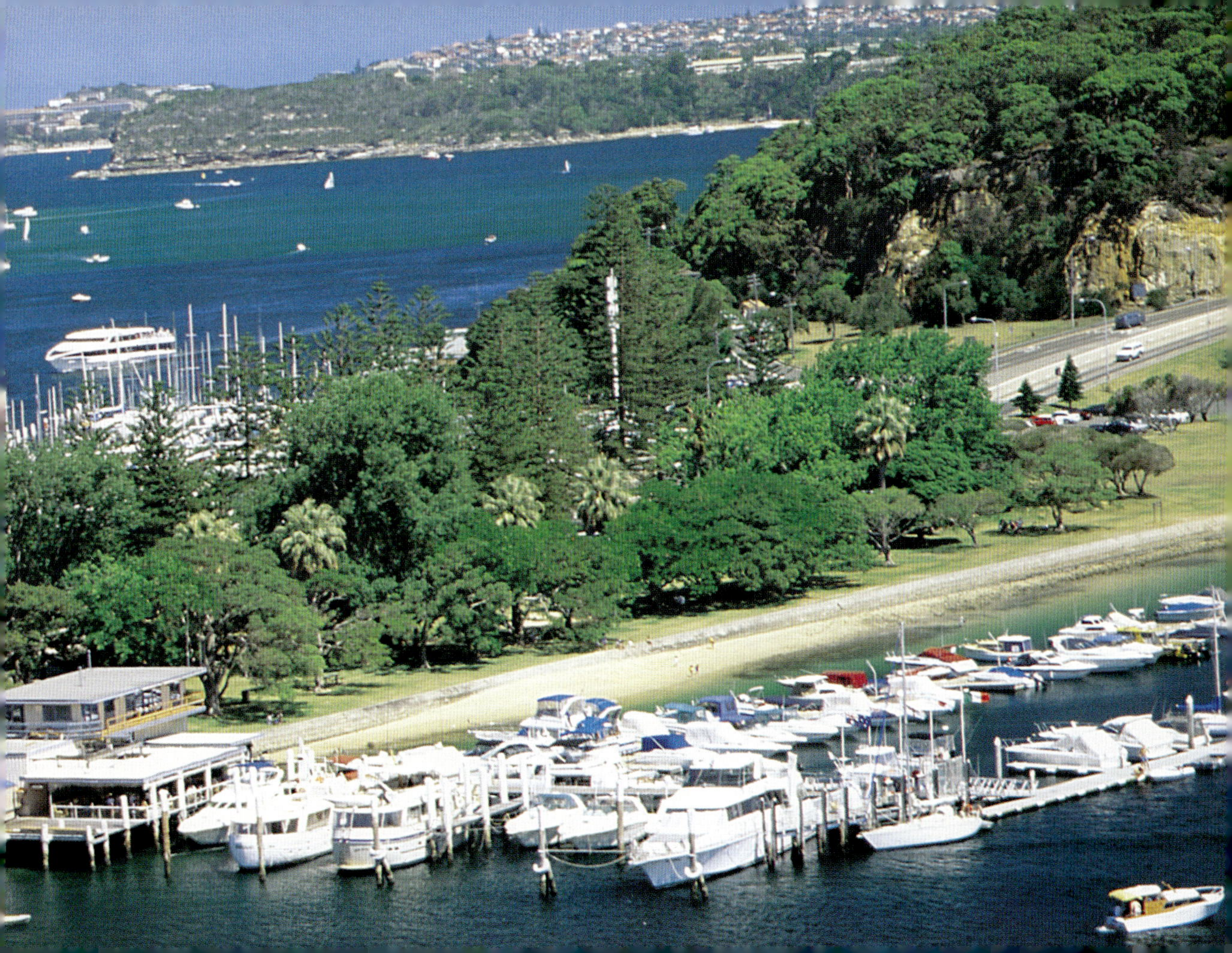

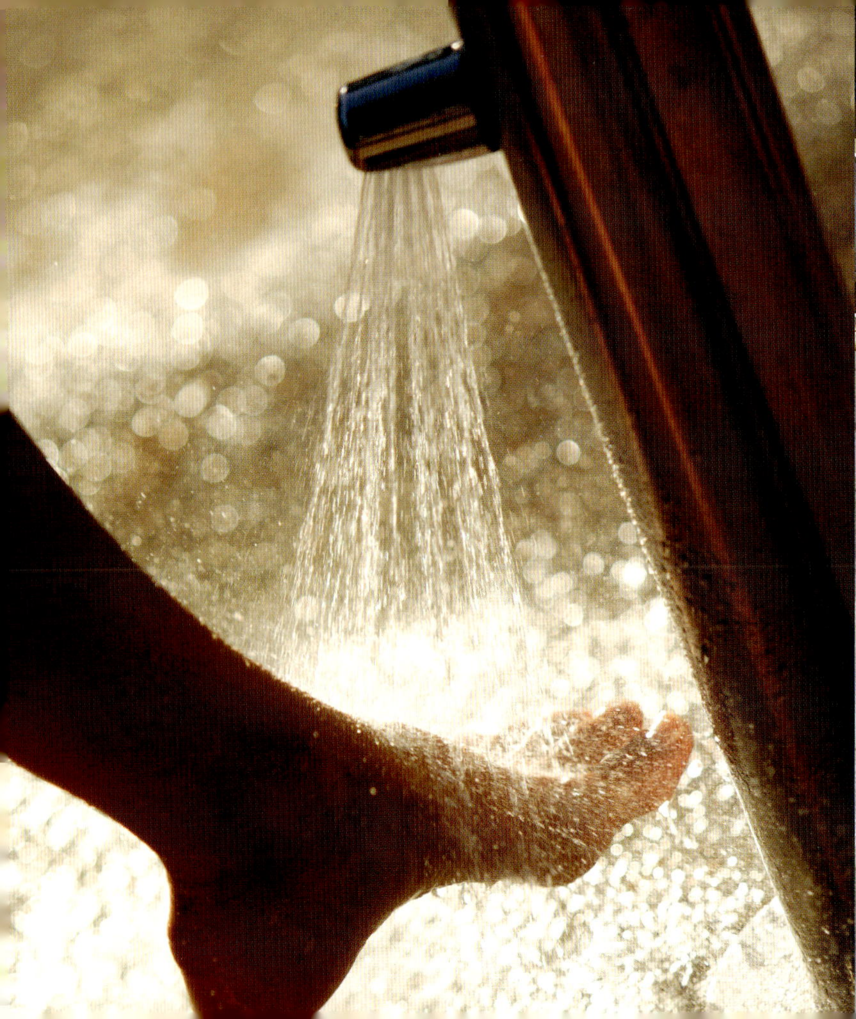
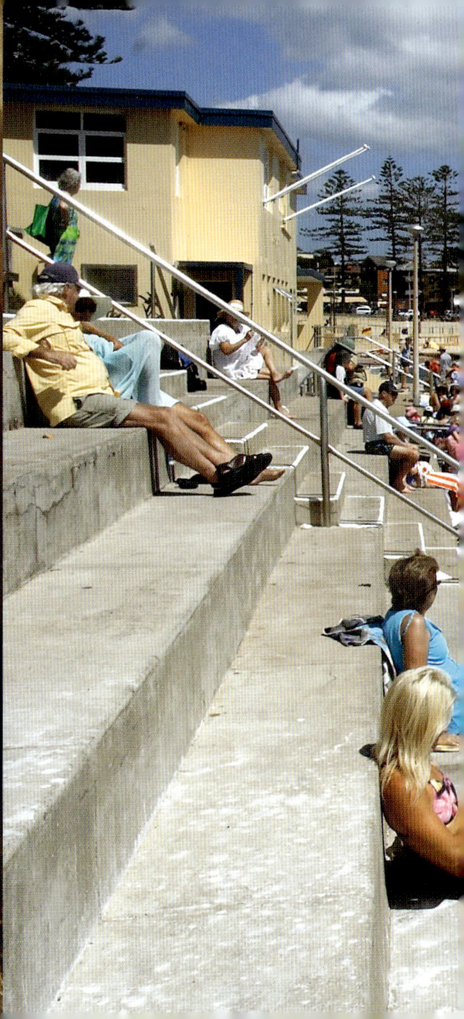

Dee Why's oceanside pools are popular with families and lap swimmers   43

The view from Mosman across the Harbour to the Sydney skyline

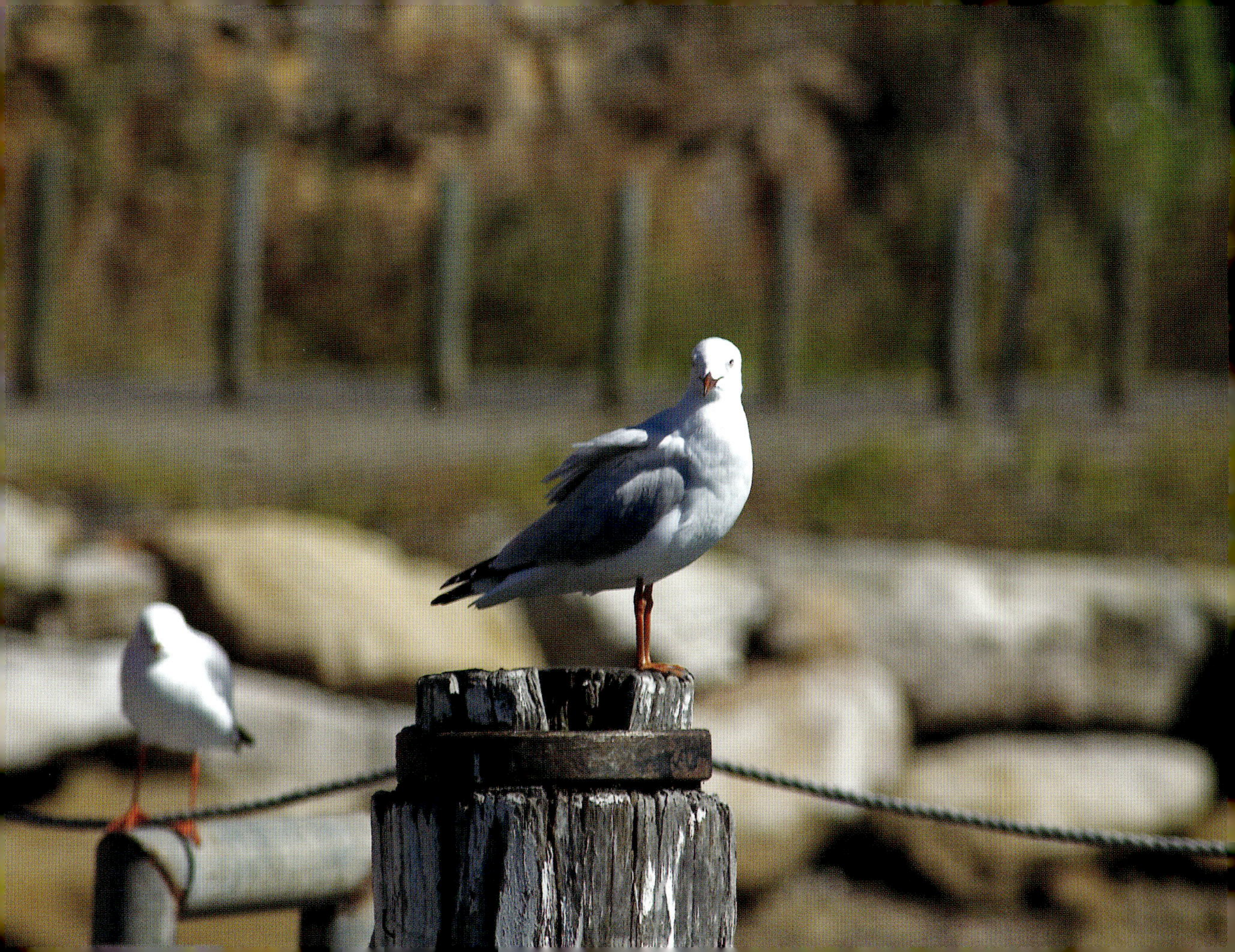

Swimming is a big part of life for most Australians from childhood

The famous Bondi Baths attract lap swimmers even in the coldest winter months

Federation Cliff Walk, Vaucluse

Bondi Beach is easily accessible from the city centre

50 Lifesavers compete with other surf clubs to stay in top form

Beachgoers are encouraged to swim in the patrolled area between the flags for their own safety

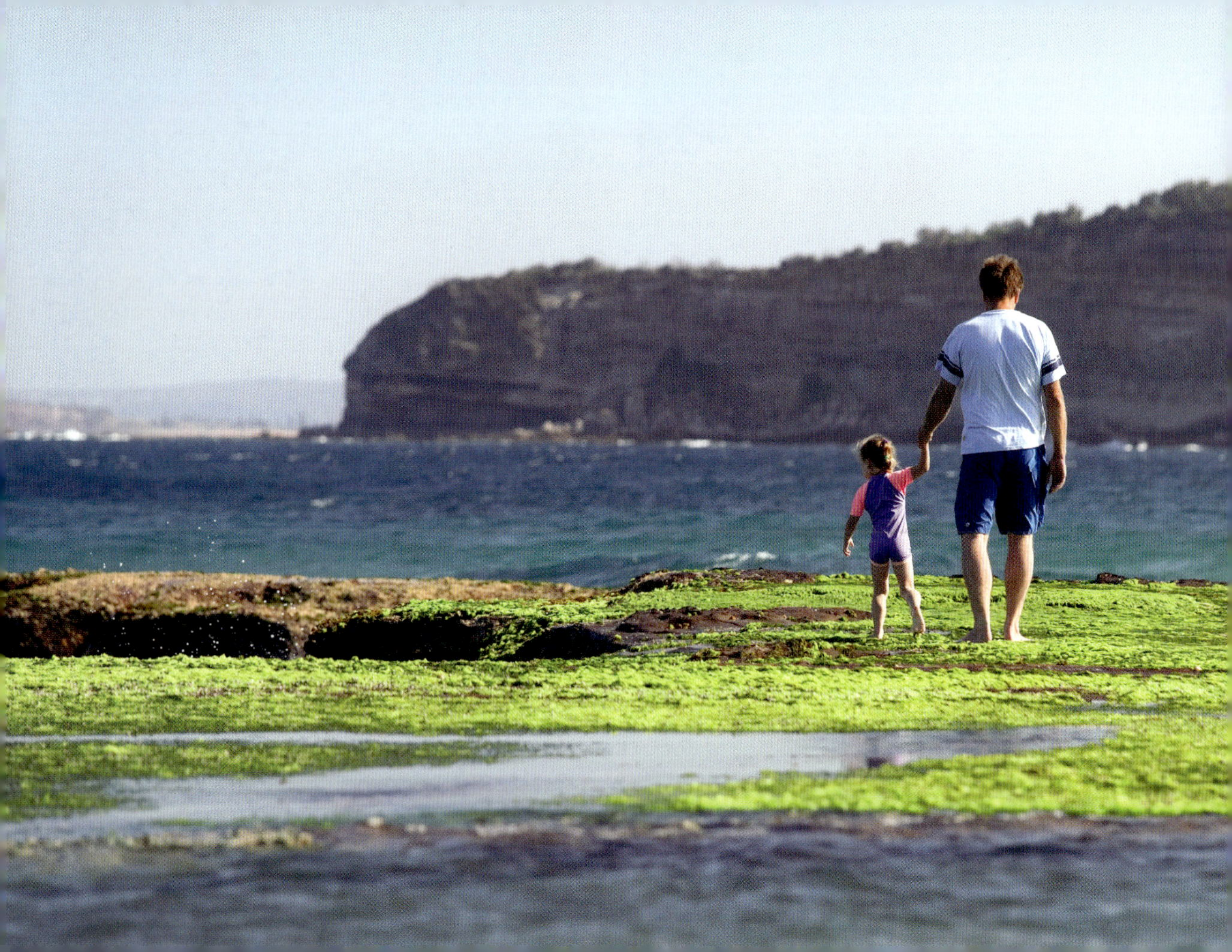

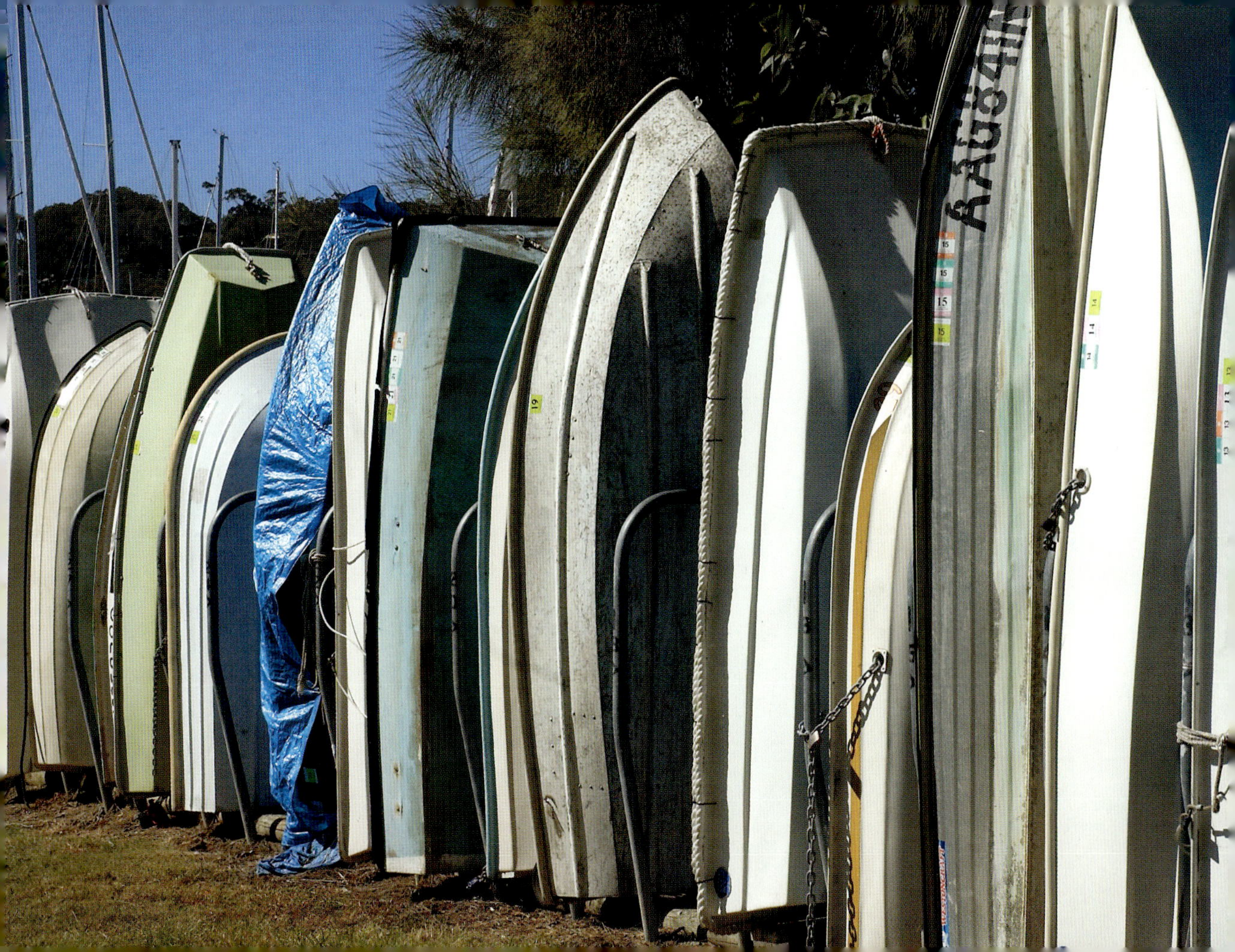

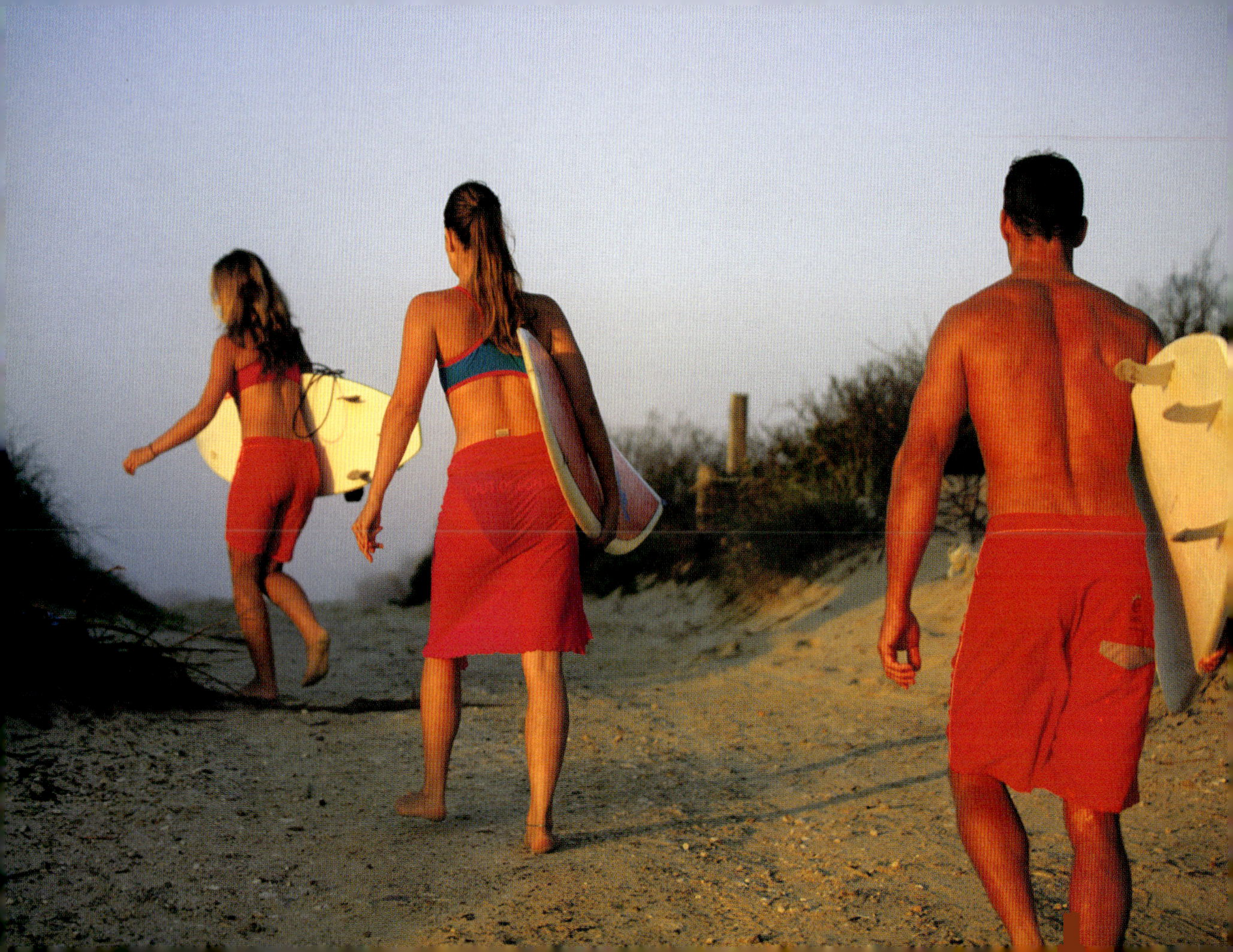

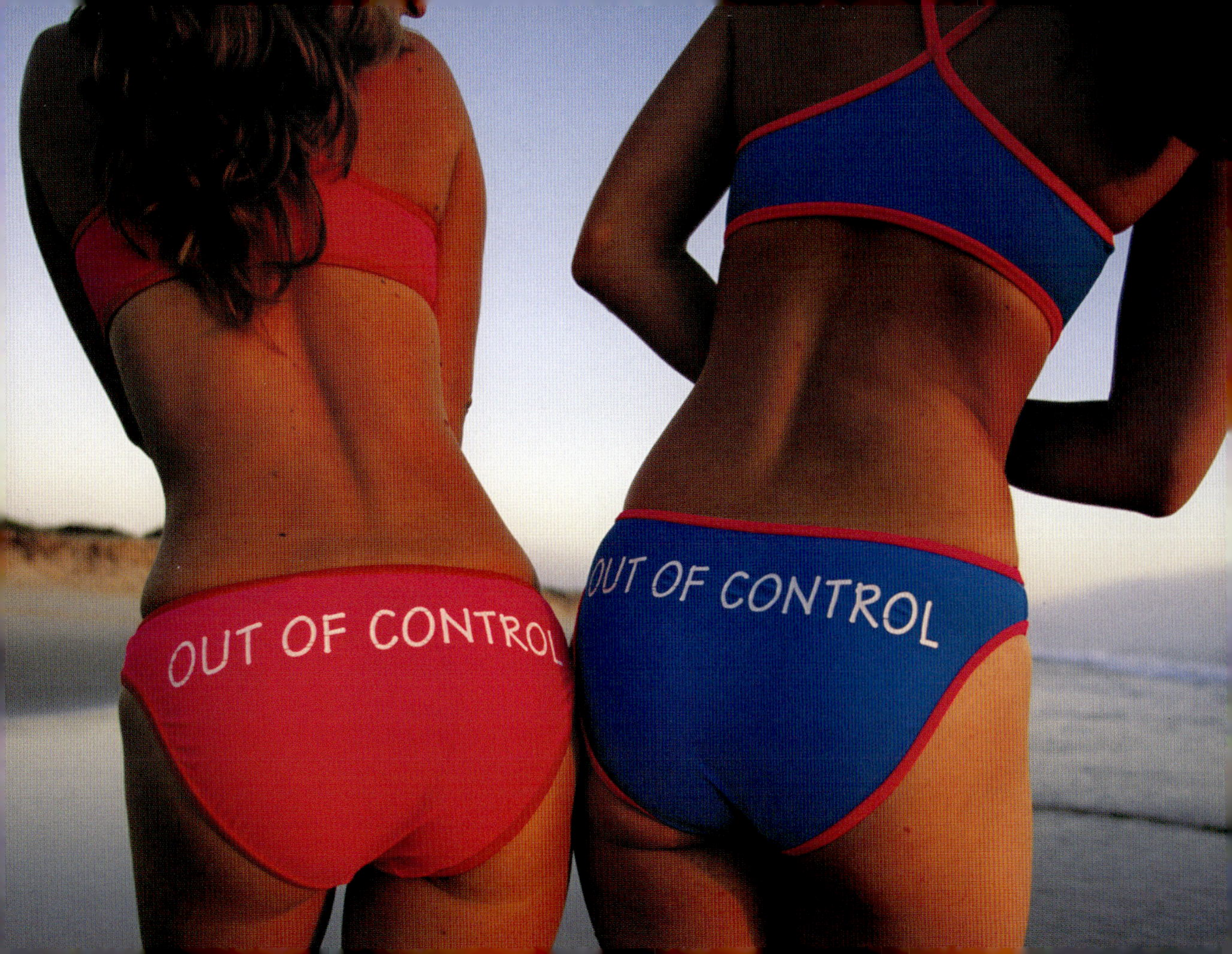
OUT OF CONTROL
OUT OF CONTROL

56 It is a lifelong quest for many surfers to ride the perfect wave

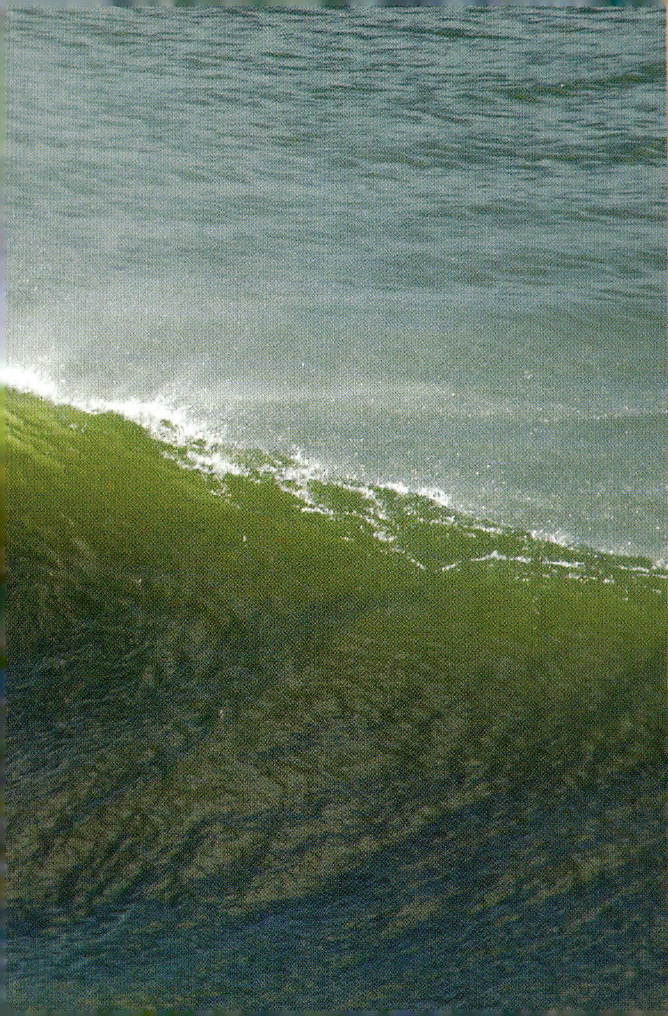
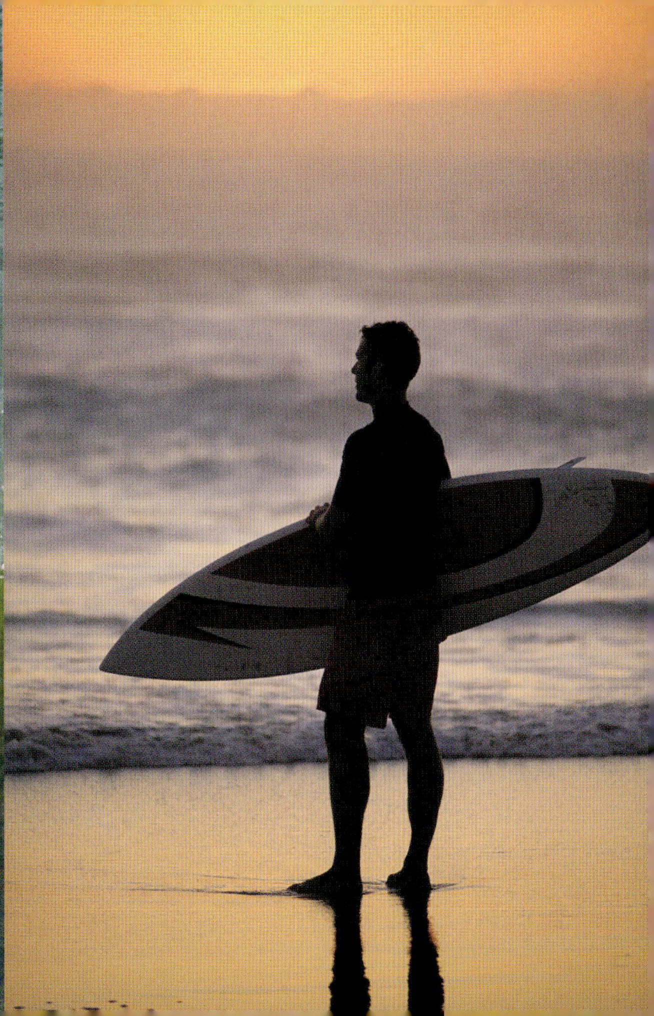

Byron Bay in northern New South Wales
Next page: Wattegoes Beach provides a good location for an impromptu game of cricket

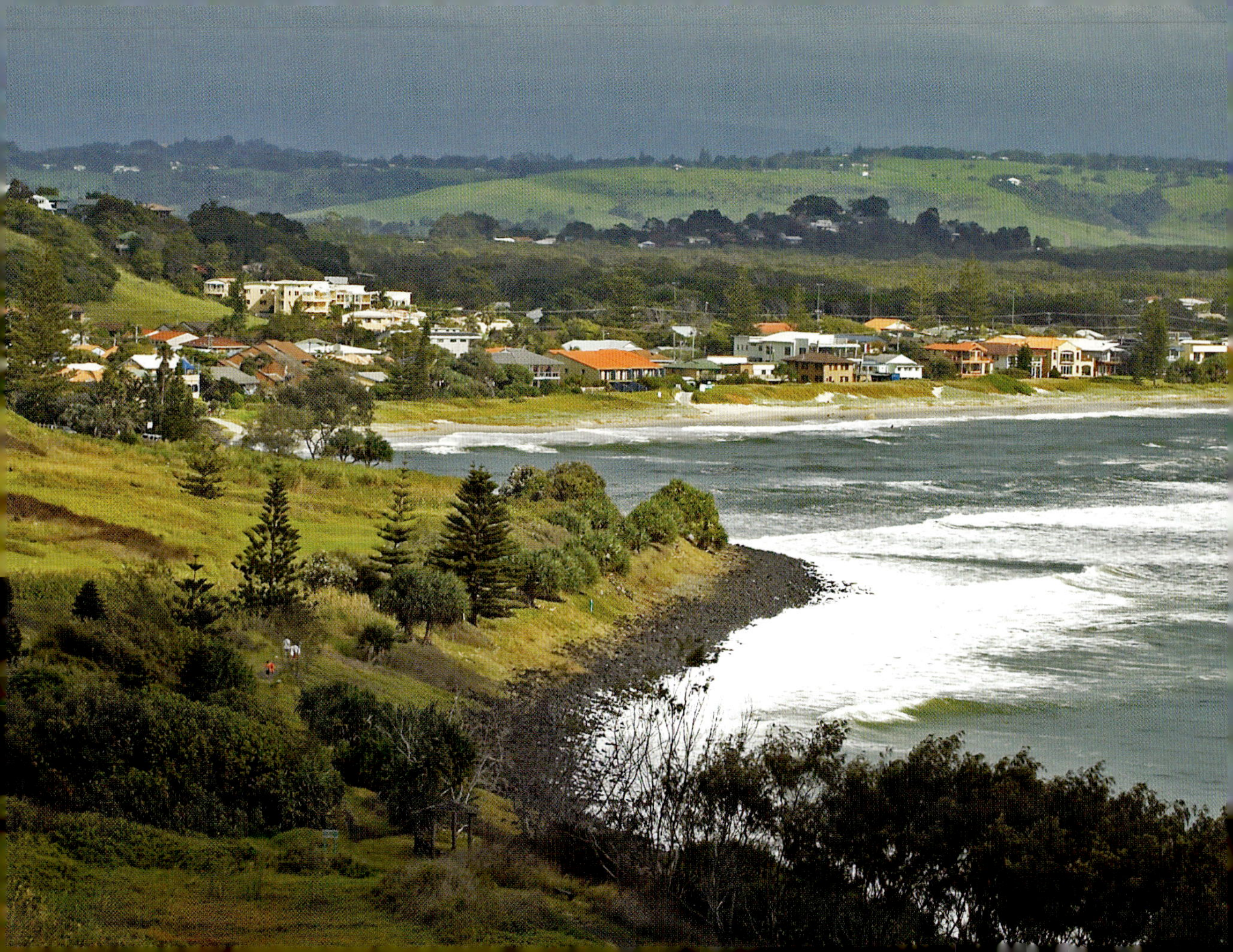

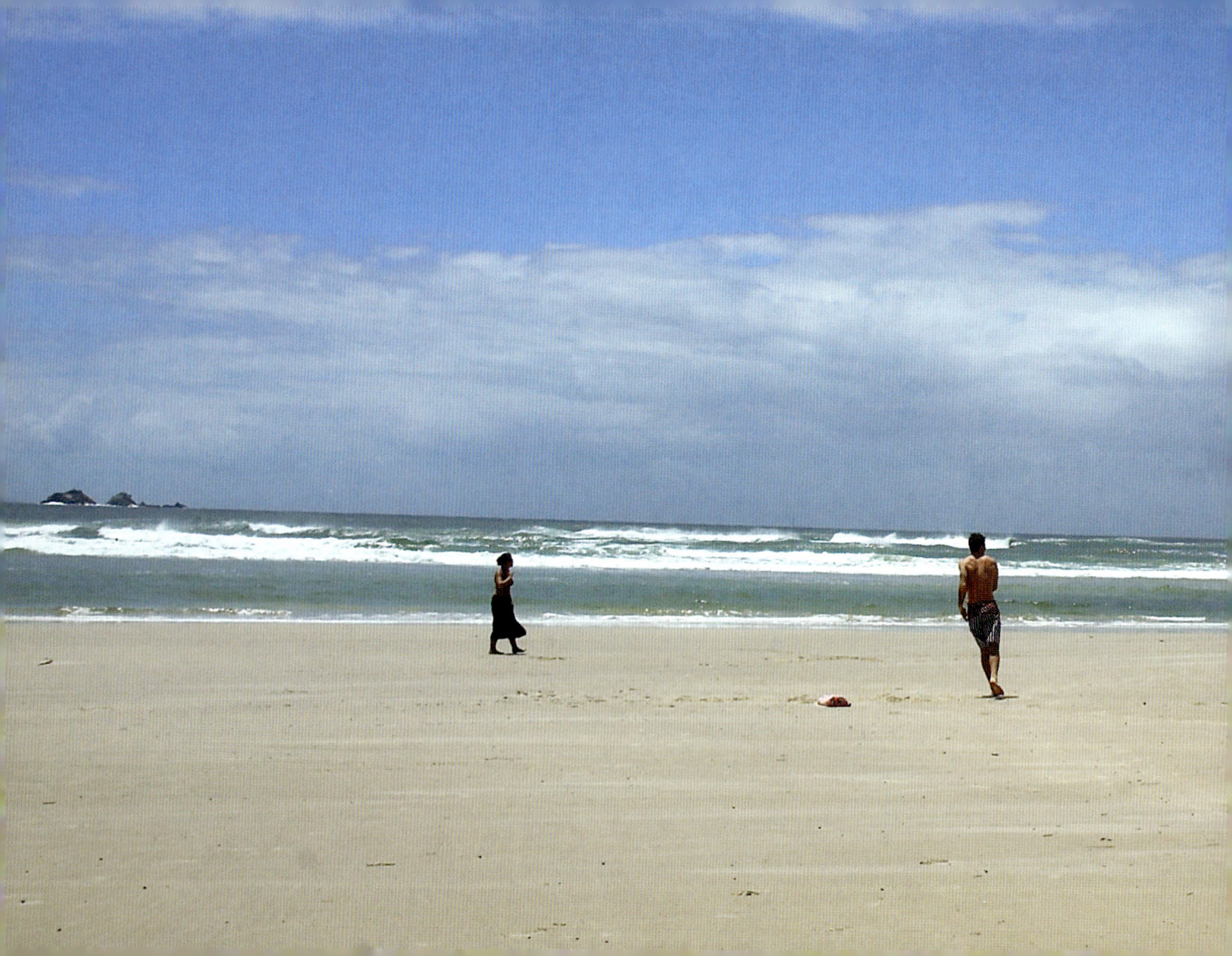

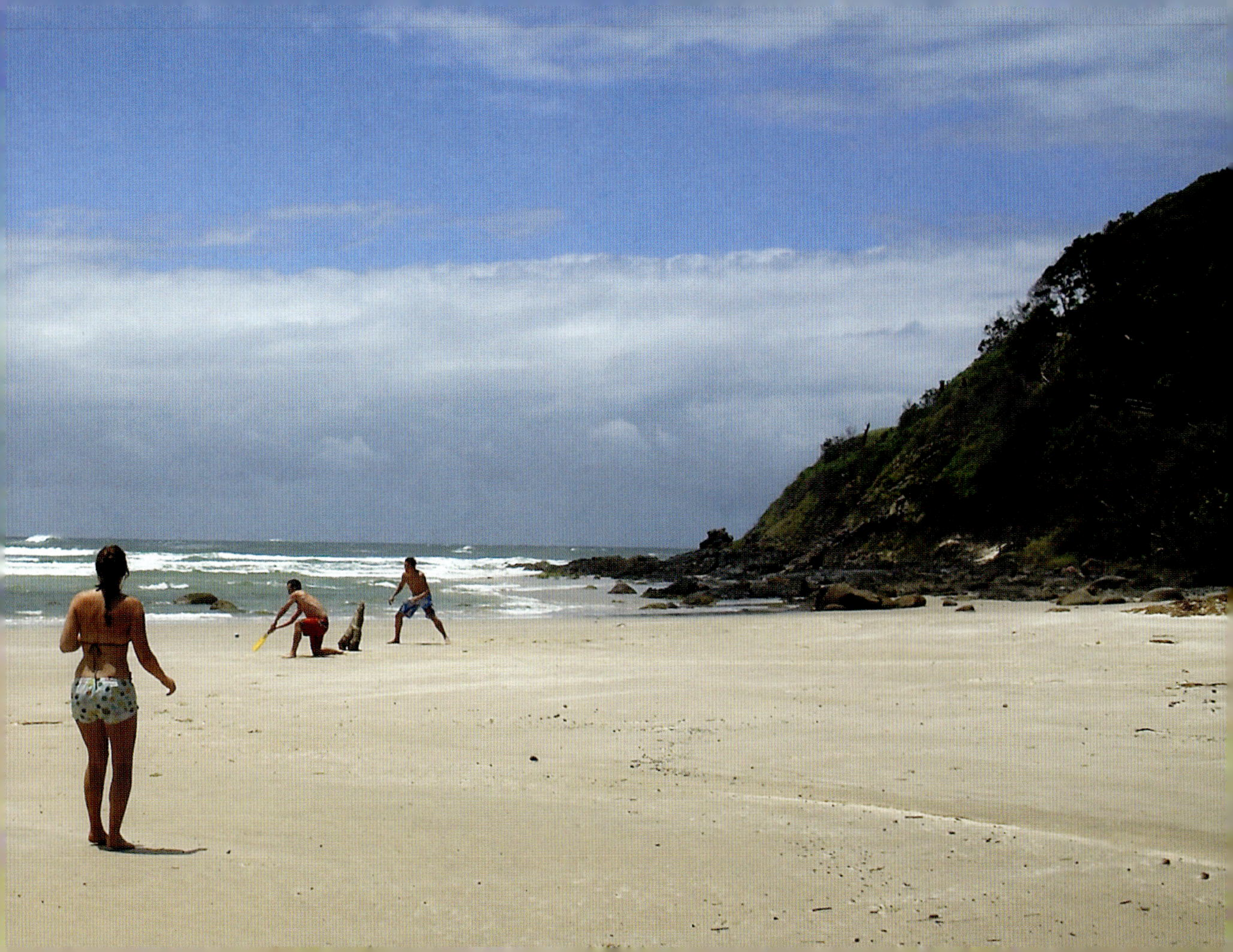

Fishing off the jetty at South West Rocks

Kayaking on the tranquil Lake Jindabyne on the eastern slopes of the Snowy Mountains

Horse riding in Millamolong in central New South Wales

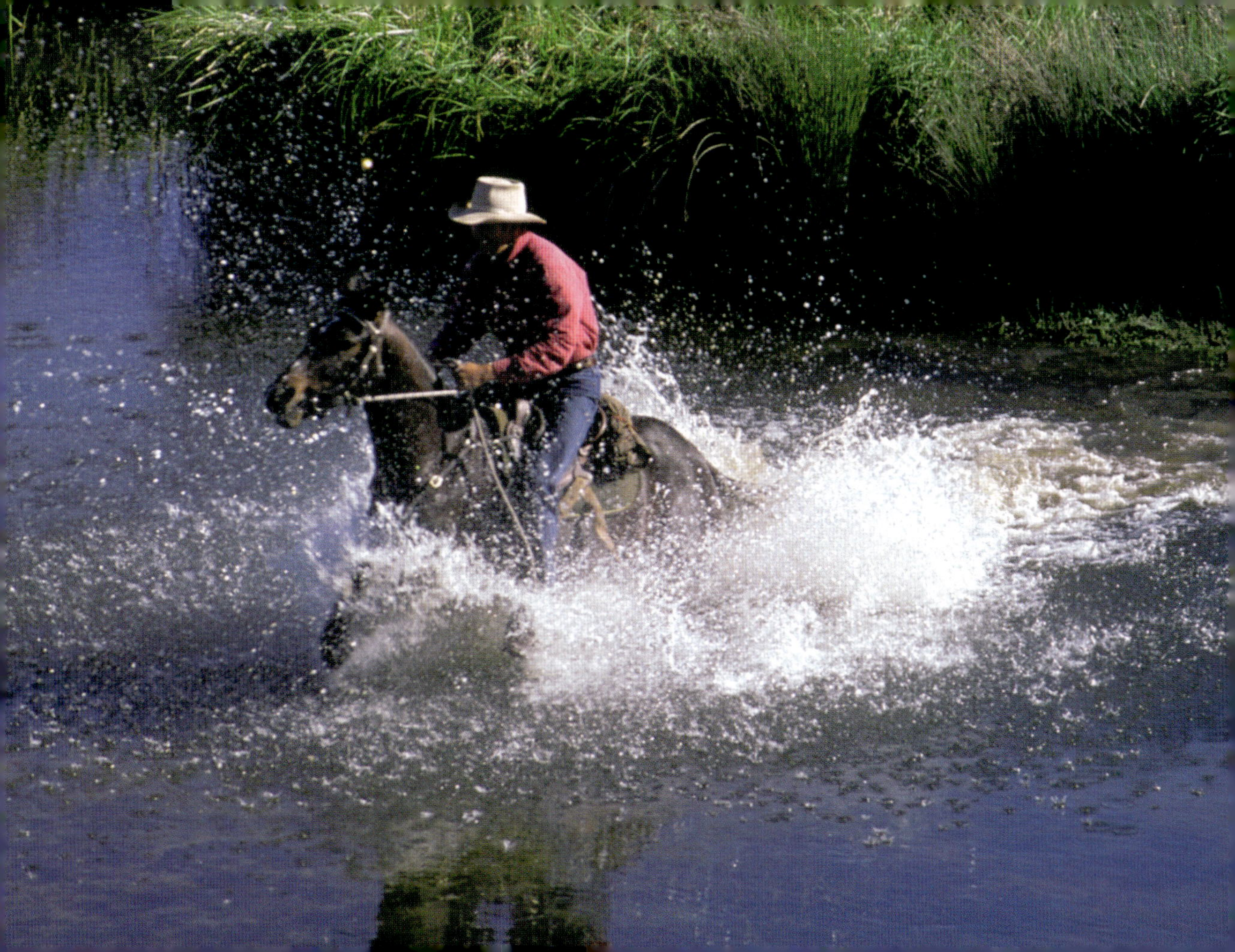

66 Port Stephens is a dream come true for pelicans

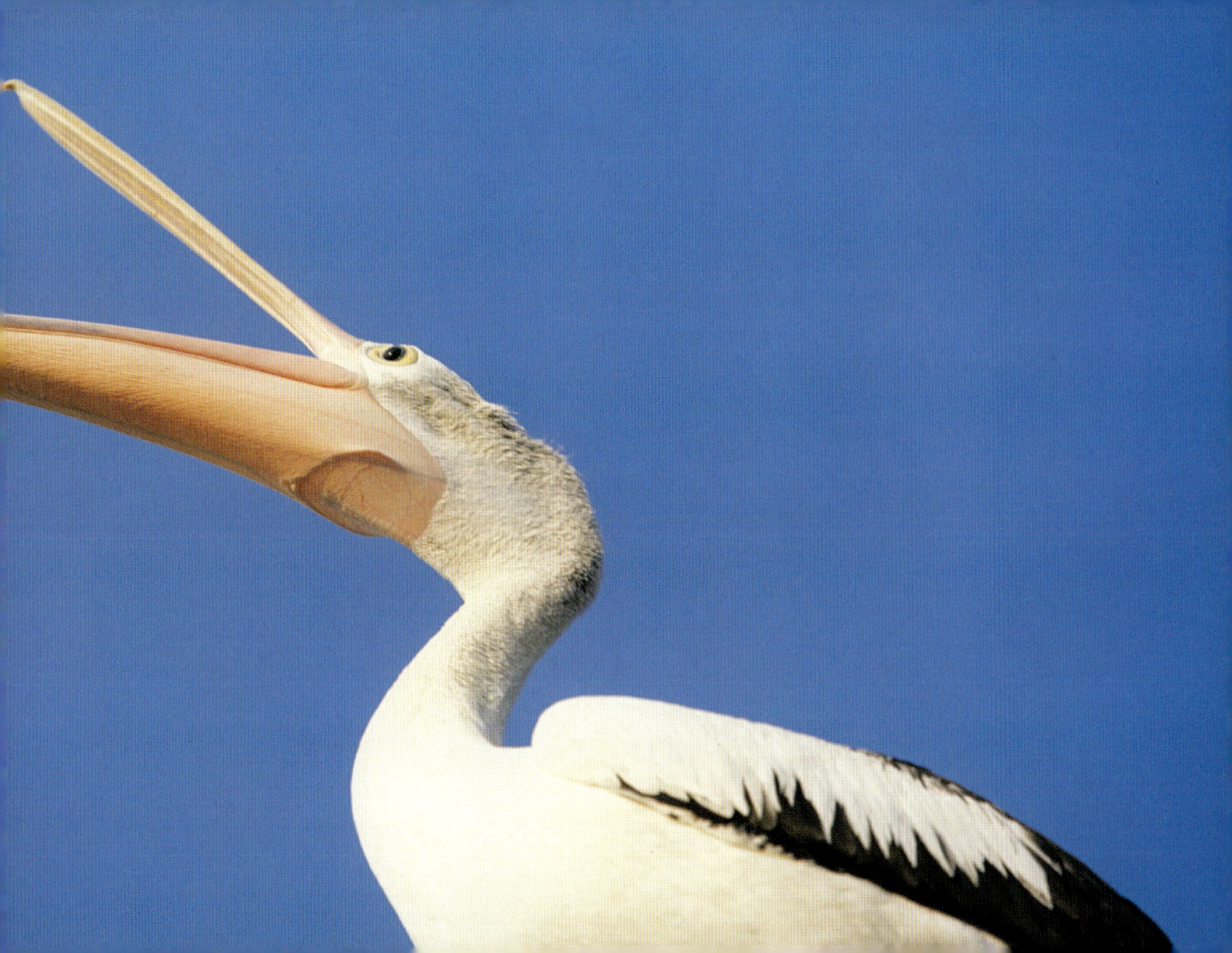

68 | This hut in the Blue Mountains is typical of the architecture in the early years of Australian settlement

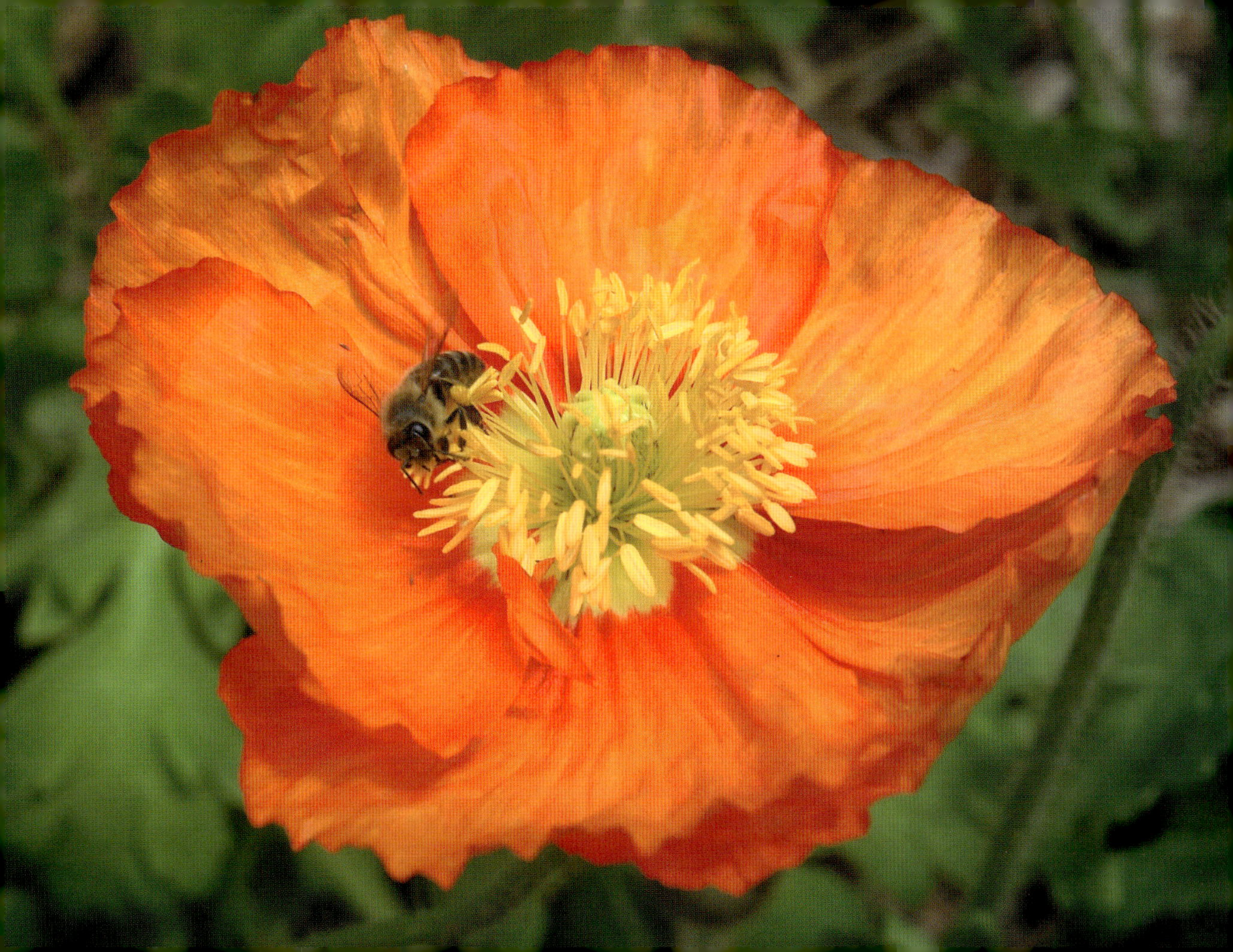

70   Tourists get a bird's-eye view of the Blue Mountains escarpment

Lithgow's Zig-zag Railway was a 19th century engineering feat. Next page: the ever-changing colours of the Blue Mountains

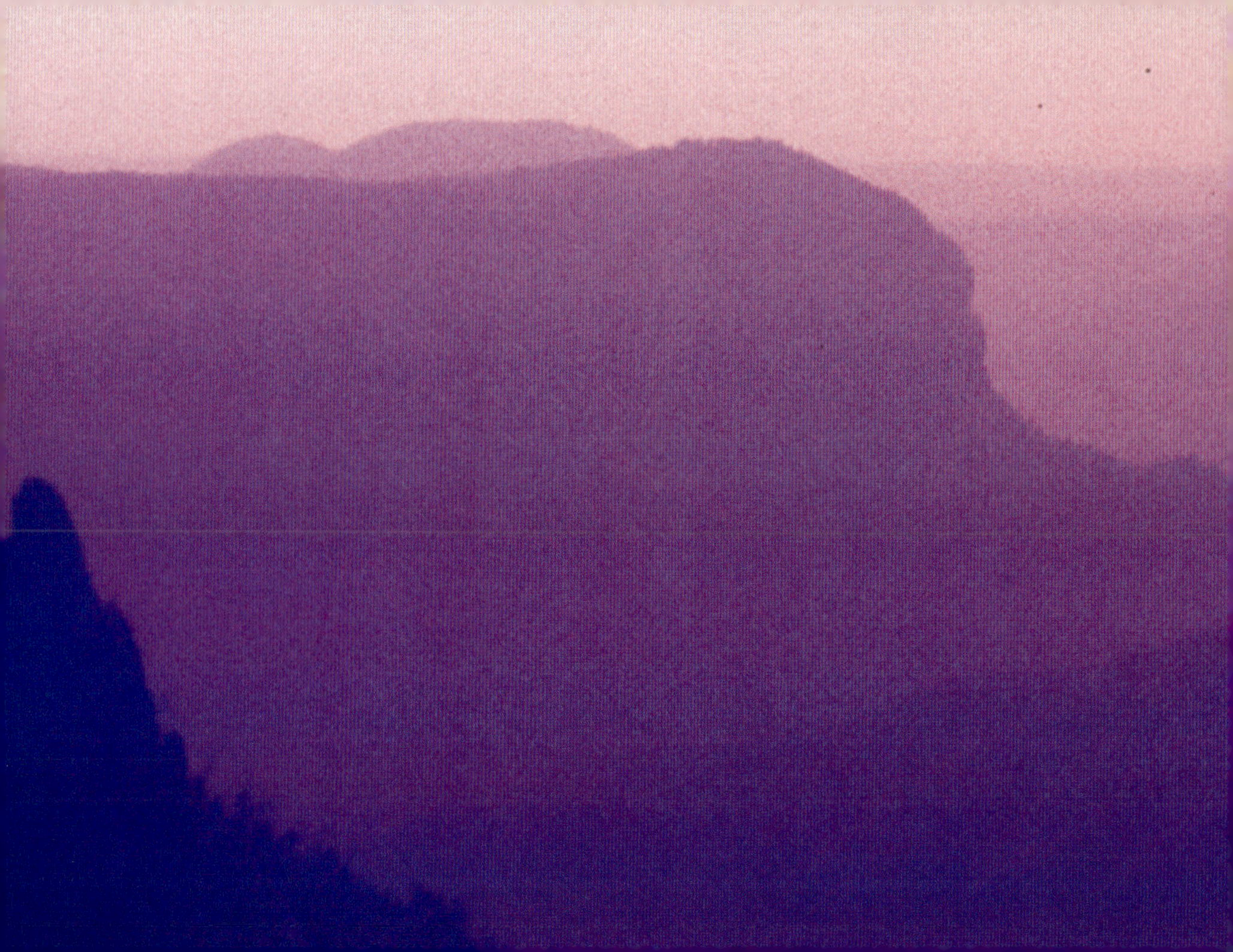

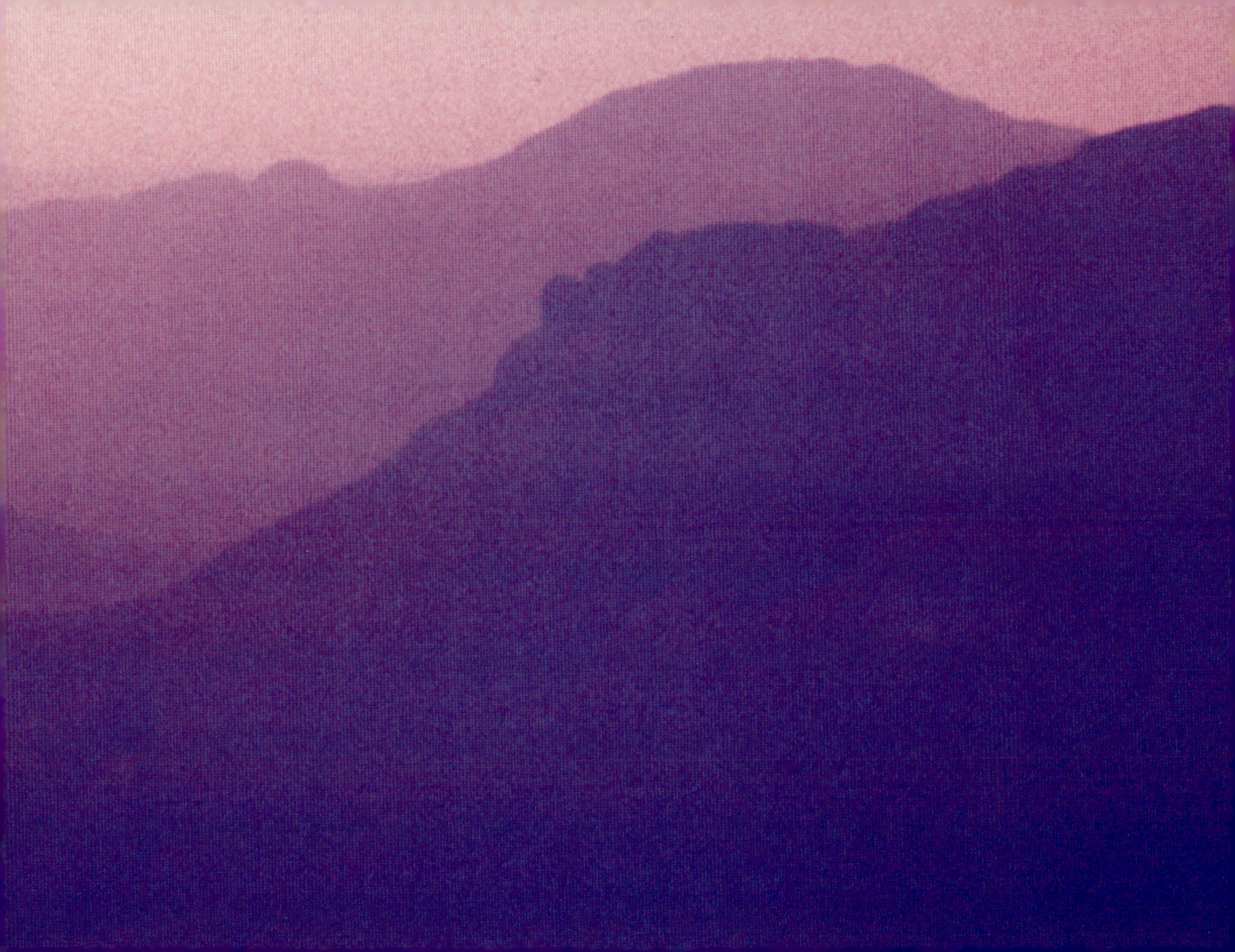

74 Katoomba is a town perched high in the Blue Mountains

The Three Sisters is a rock formation best seen from Katoomba

76 Giant ferns in the Blue Mountains National Park

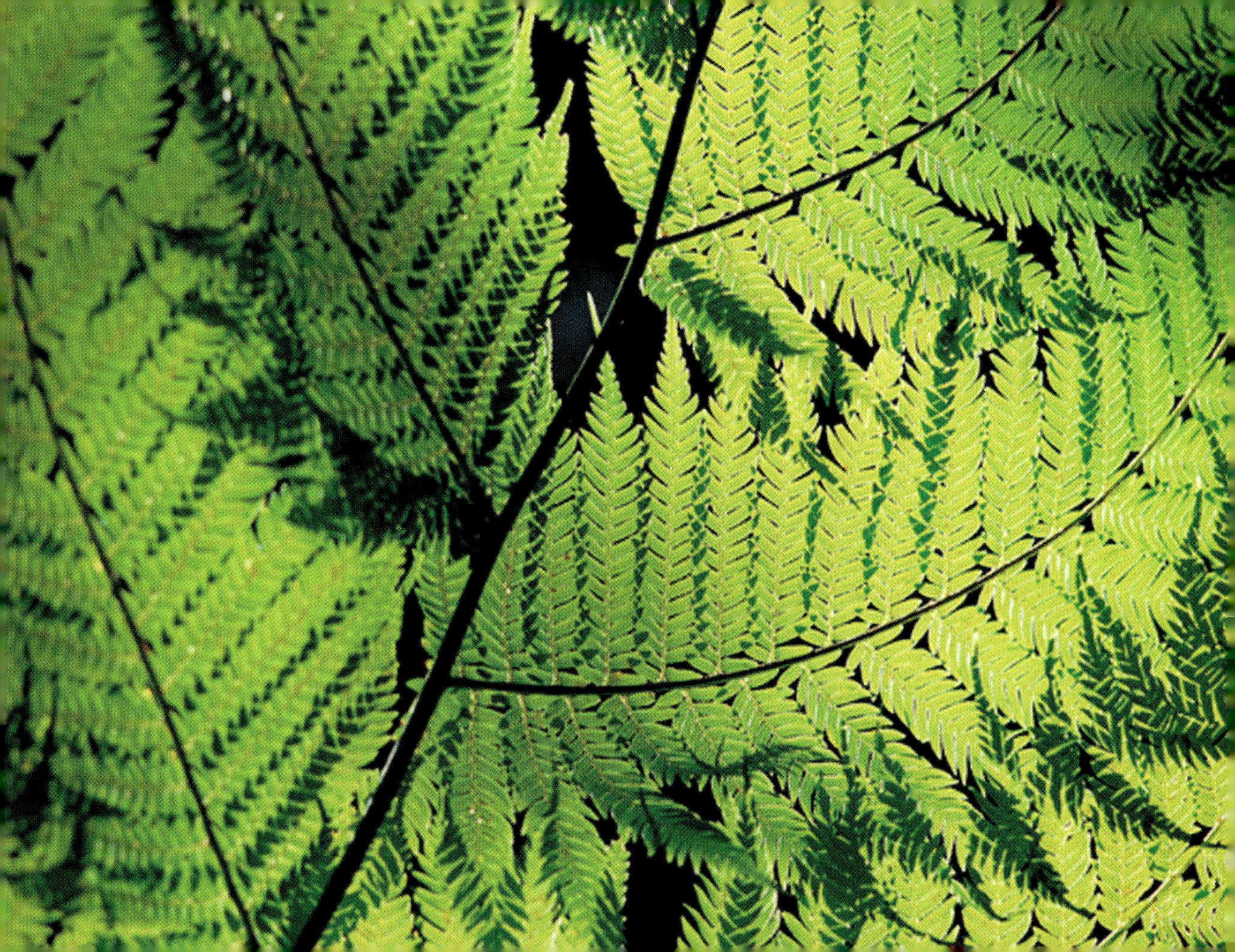

78   Leura is a popular weekend destination for its unique galleries, boutiques and shops

Apple picking at one of Bilpin's orchards is a fun autumn activity   79

80 Kosciuszko National Park in the Snowy Mountains

Skiing in the Snowy Mountains 81

82 Wool remains an important industry in Australia

Sheepdogs are clever and loyal helpers on stations across Australia

Many species of kangaroo can travel at speeds of up to 70km/h

A koala and her joey

86   The kookaburra is known for its raucus laugh

A bearded dragon basks in the sun. Next page: lush countryside near Young in south-western New South Wales.

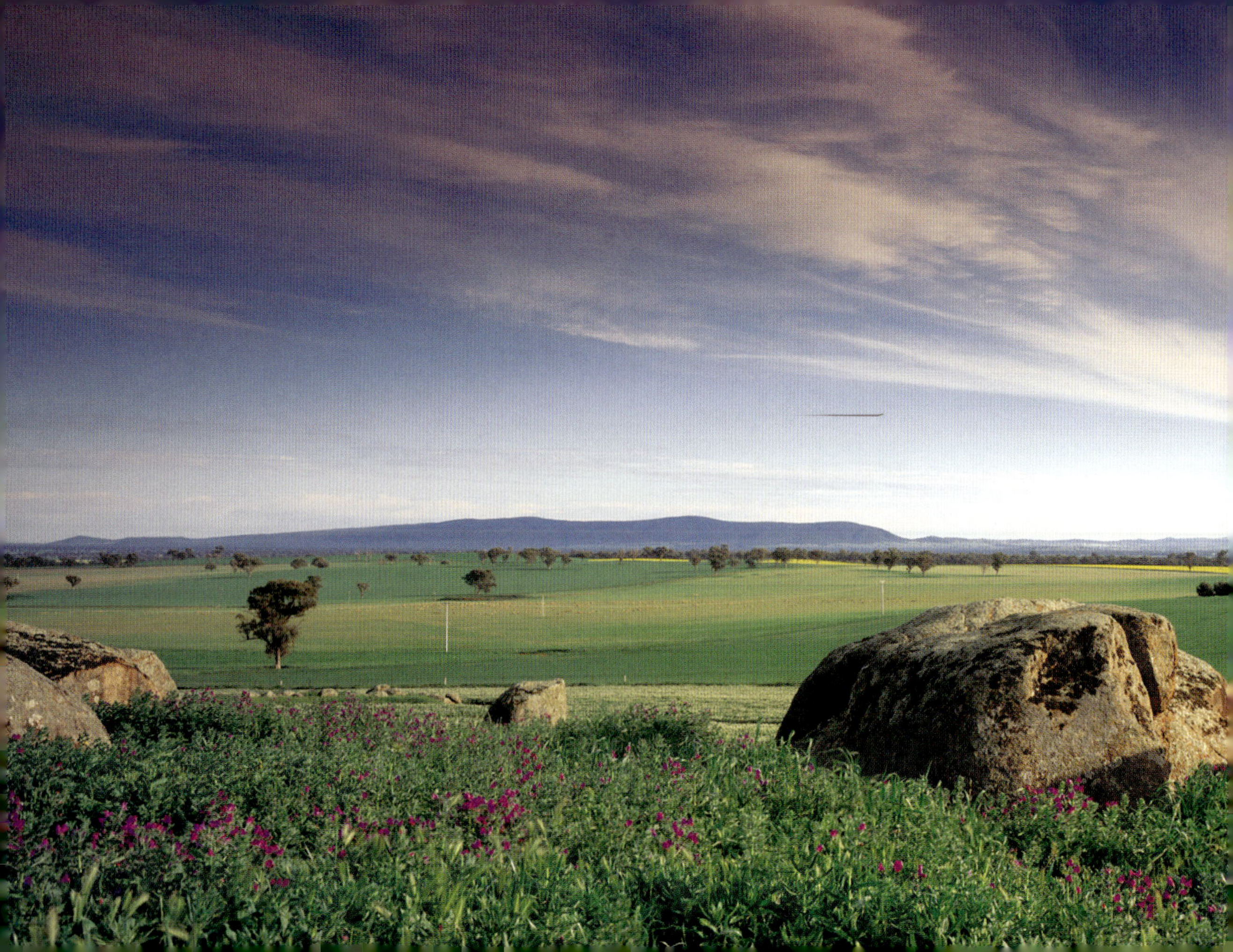

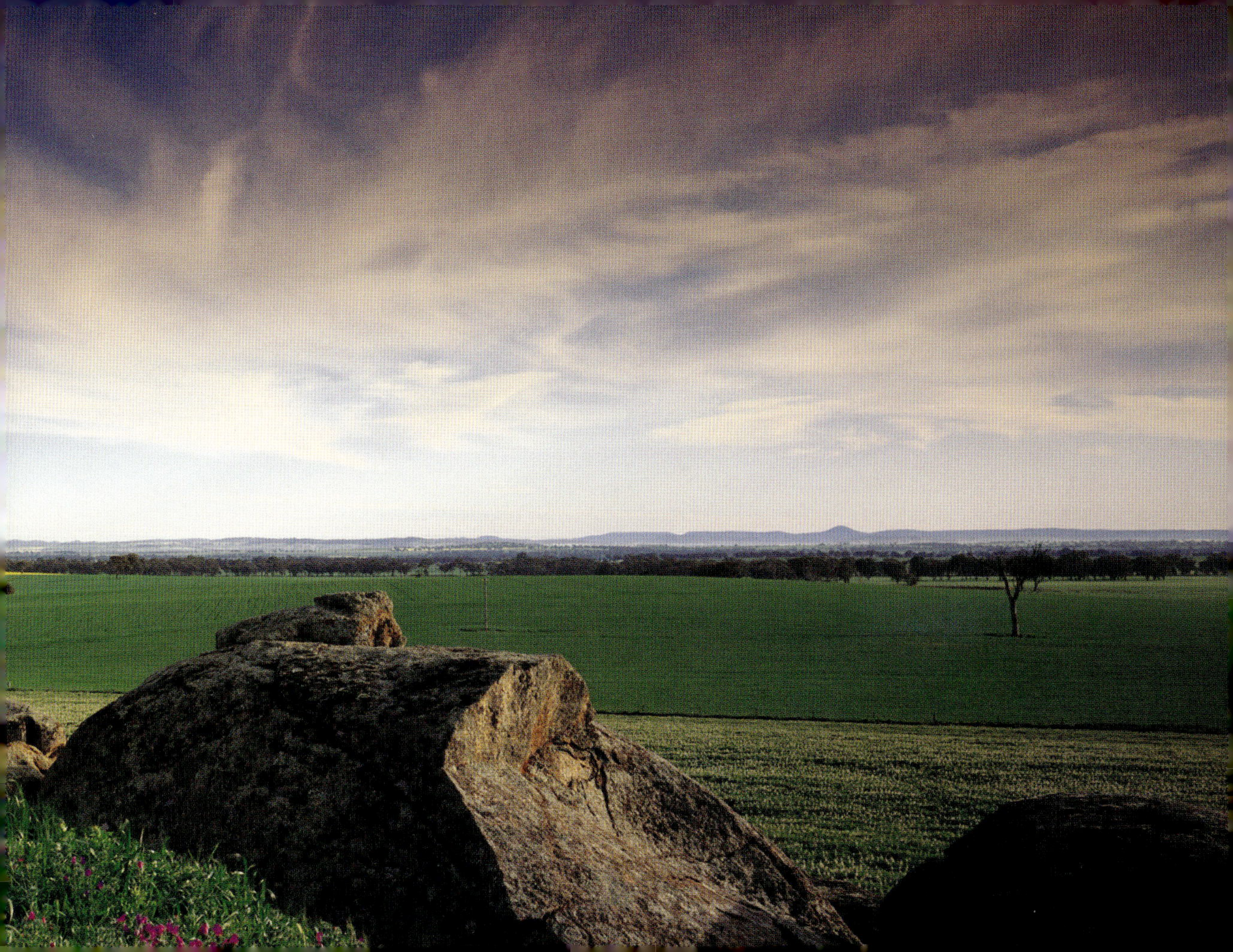

Wine produced in the Hunter Valley is exported around the world

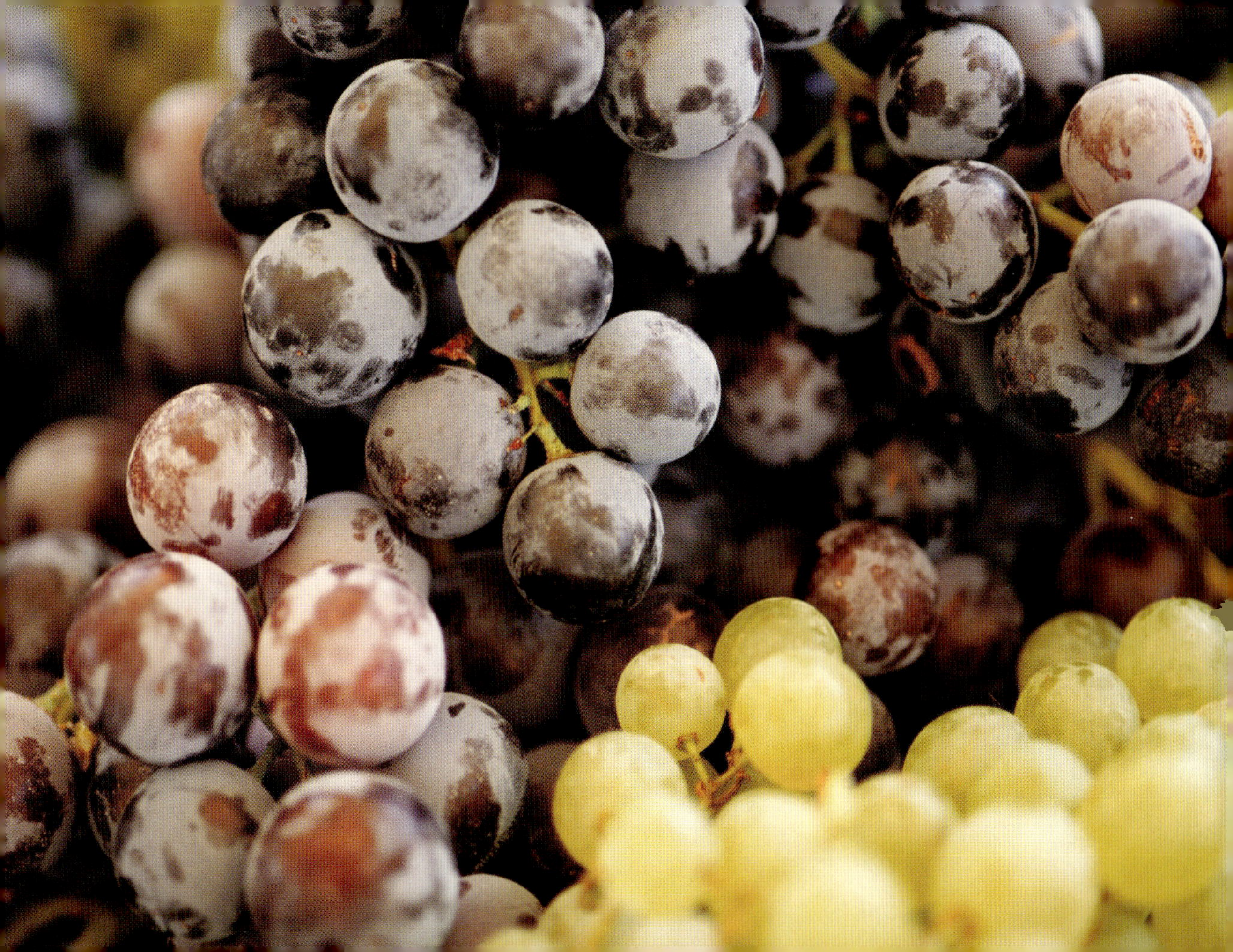

Hereford cattle are known for producing high-quality meat

Horses are used as much for work as they are for play

94 Parliament House in Canberra, the nation's capital

AUSTRALIAN CAPITAL TERRITORY

The Australian flag flies high above Parliament House 95

96 Parliament House was at the time of its construction, in 1988, the most expensive building in the Southern Hemisphere

Lake Burley Griffin is in the centre of Canberra

98 The Australian War Memorial

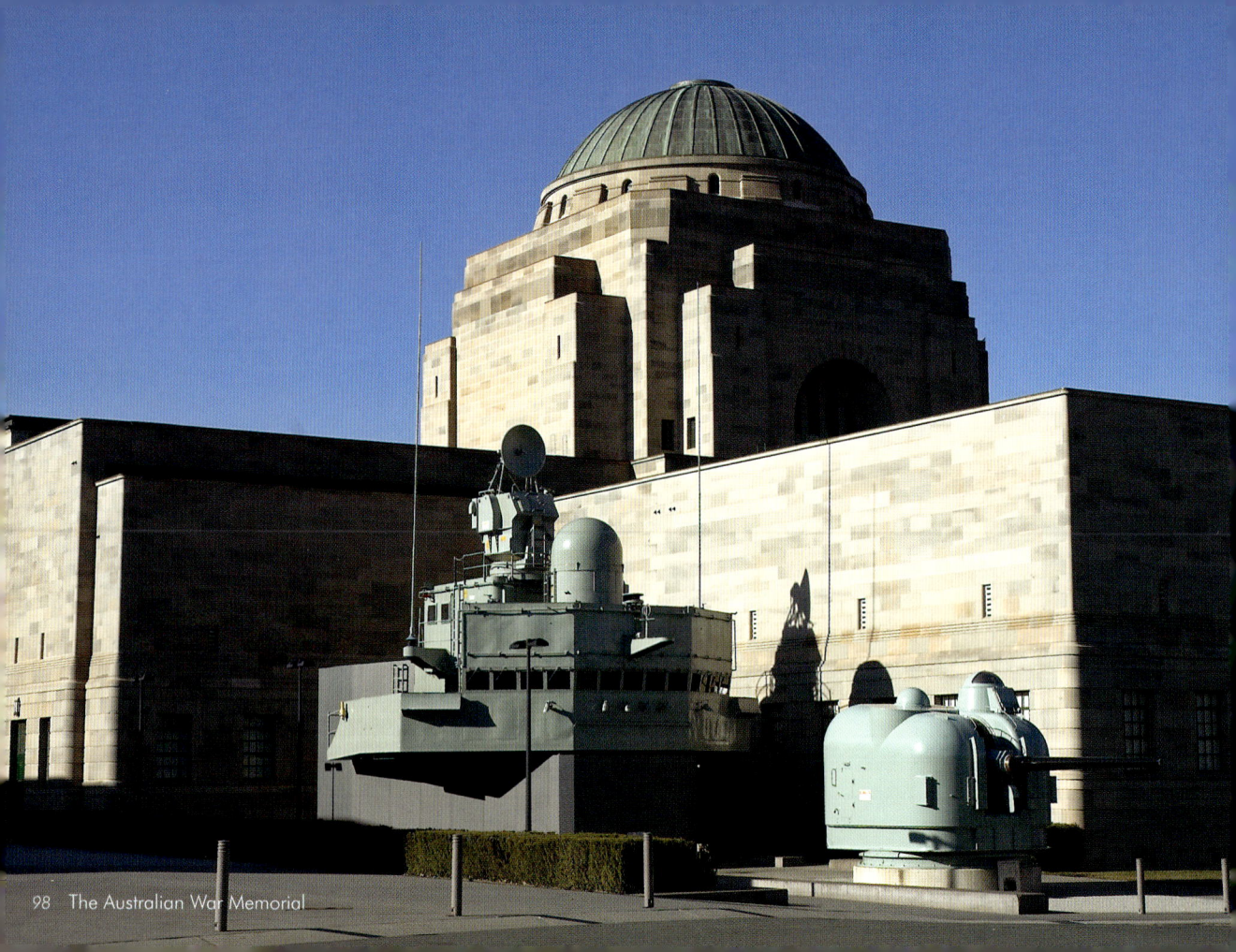

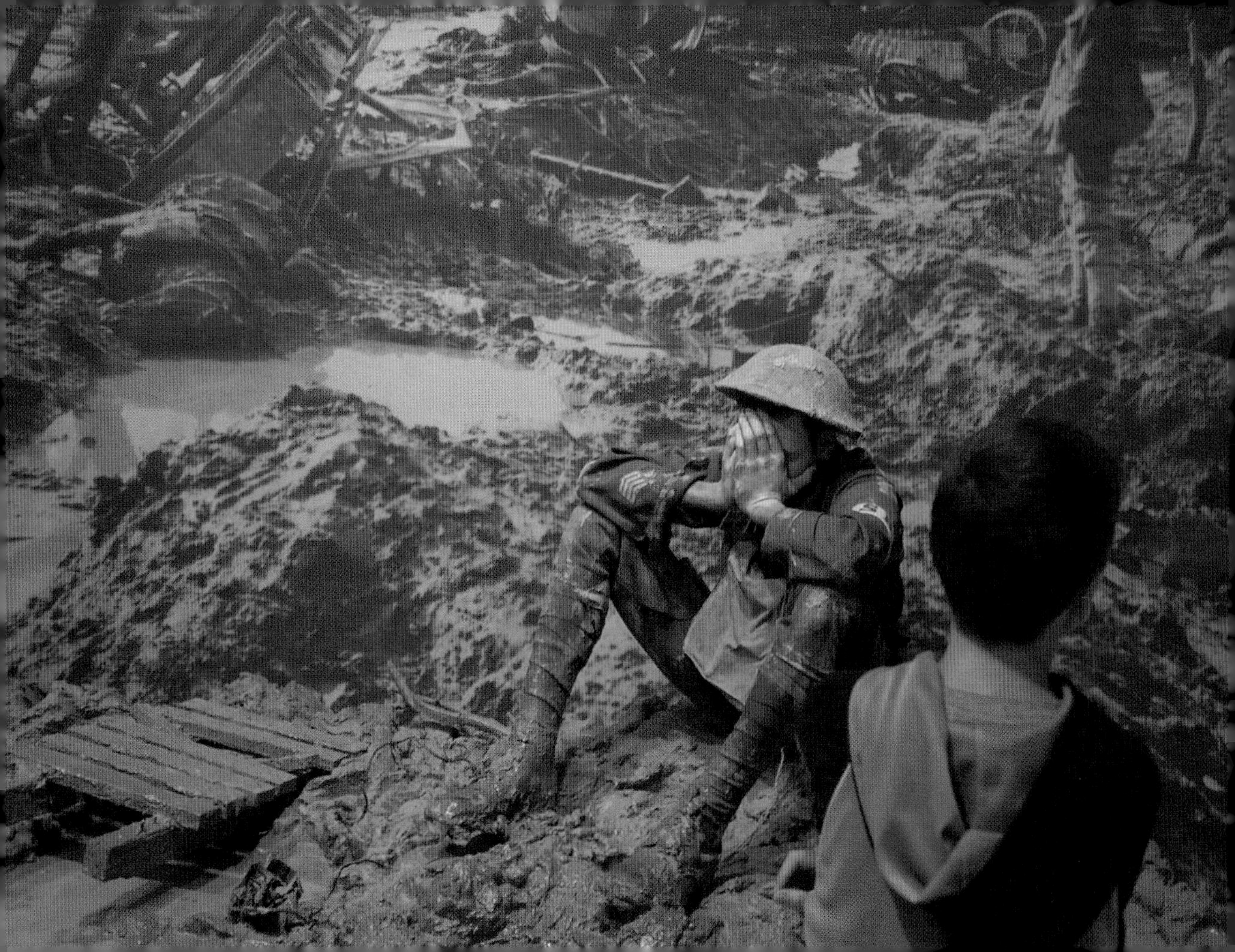

100 Canberra is known for its beautiful Autumn colours

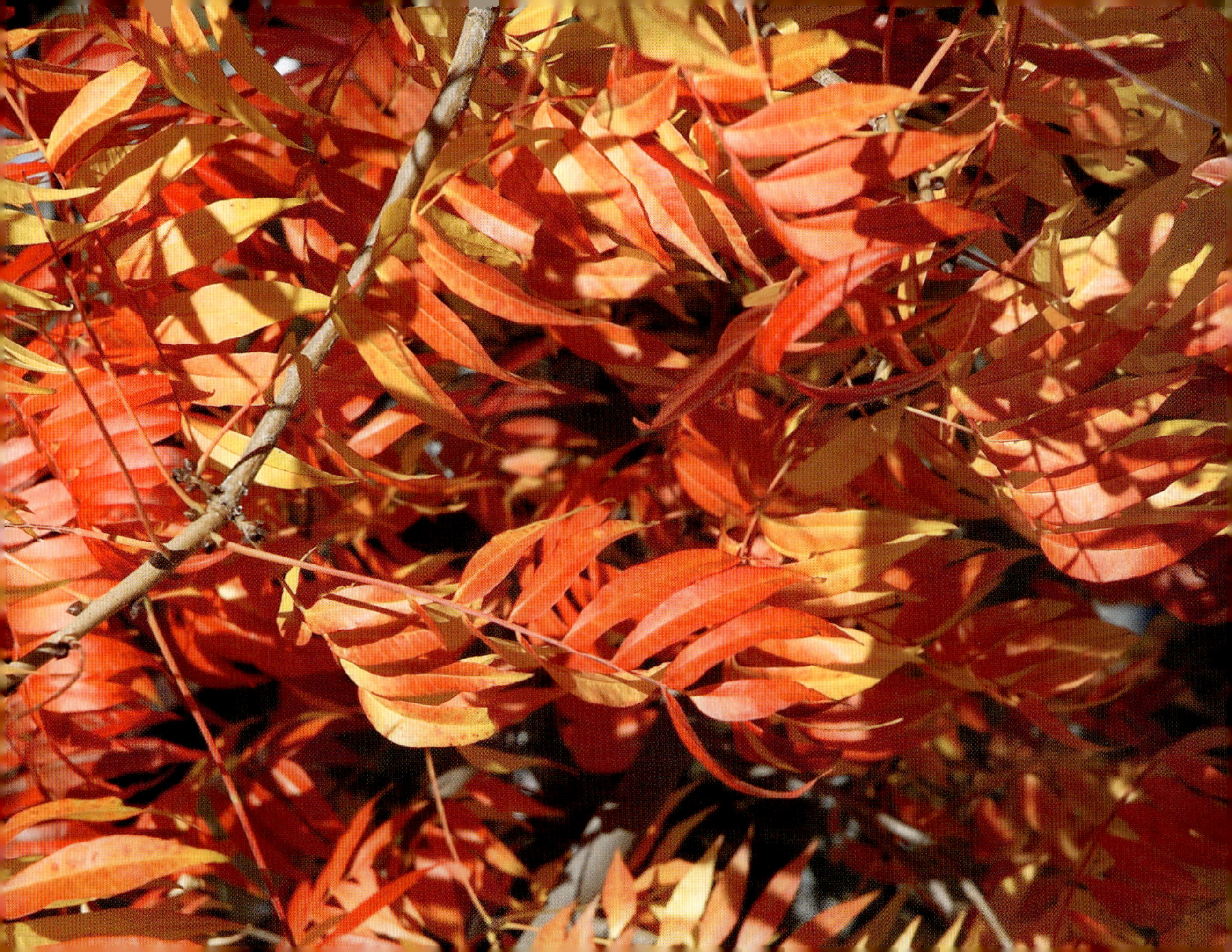

102 The National Carillion on Aspen Island chimes every quarter hour

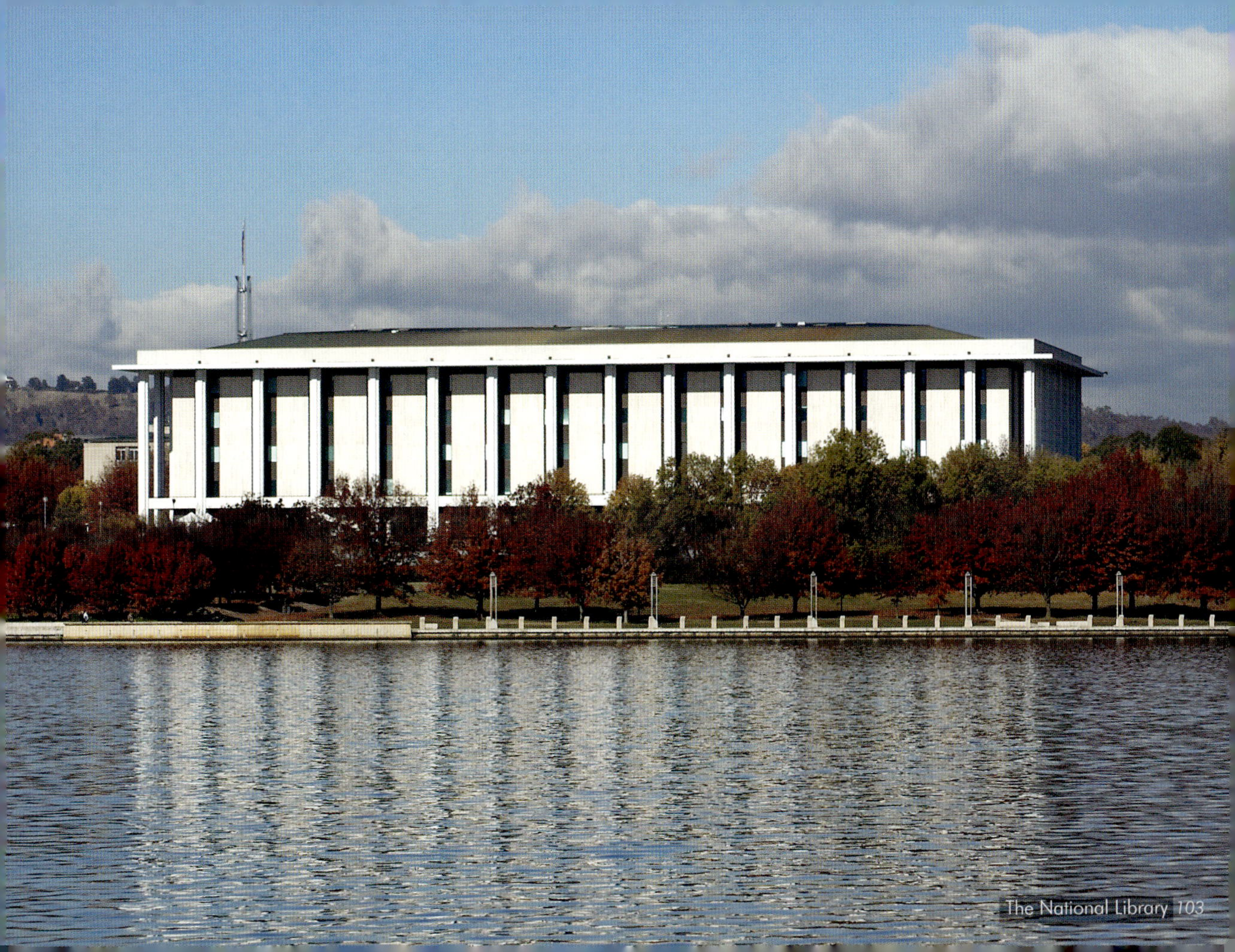

104 Melbourne's Flinders Street Station is the city's central rail hub

VICTORIA

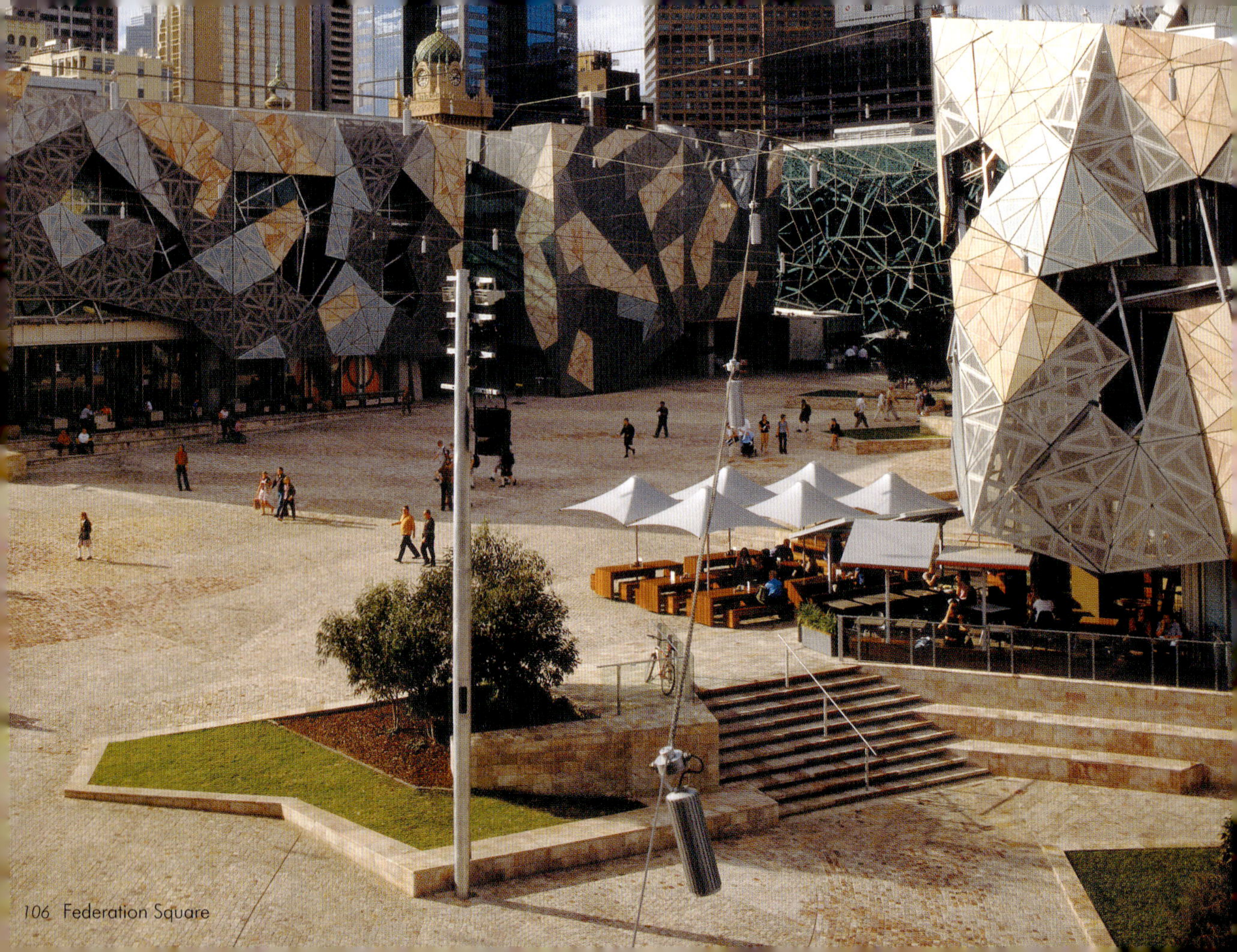

Melbourne Exhibition Centre. Next page: Melbourne at dusk

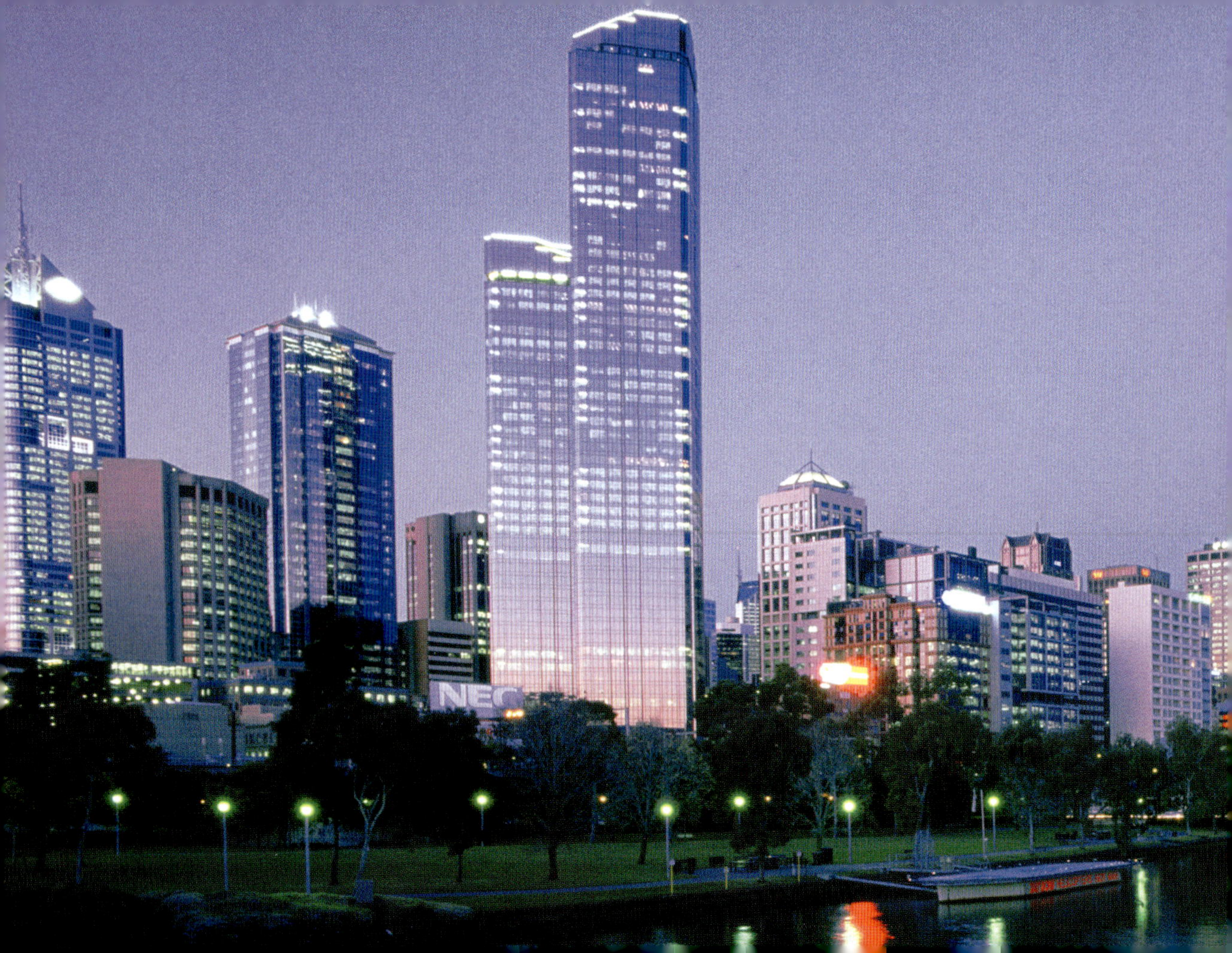
NEC

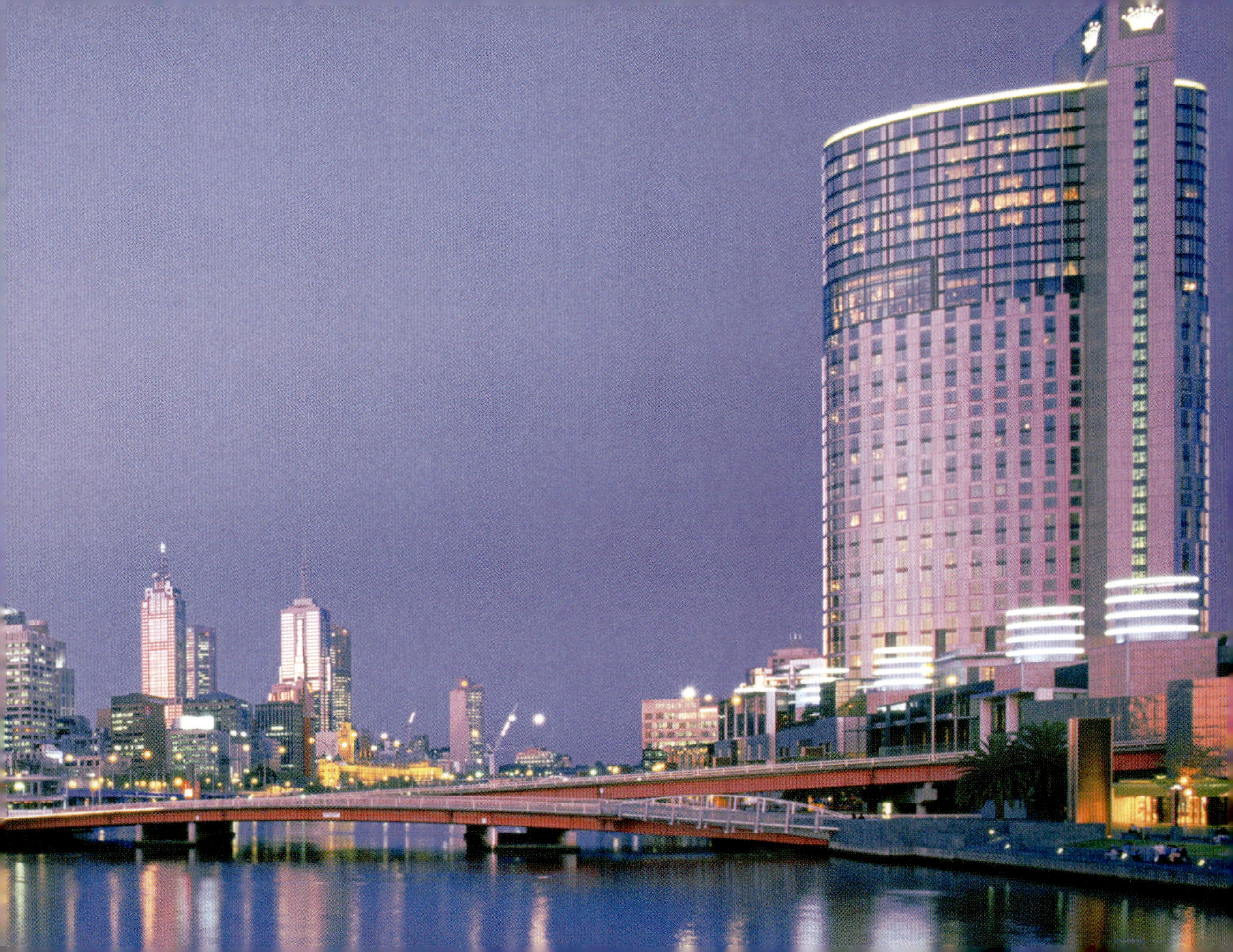

110 The Yarra River

Training at the Melbourne Cricket Ground. Next page: the city centre

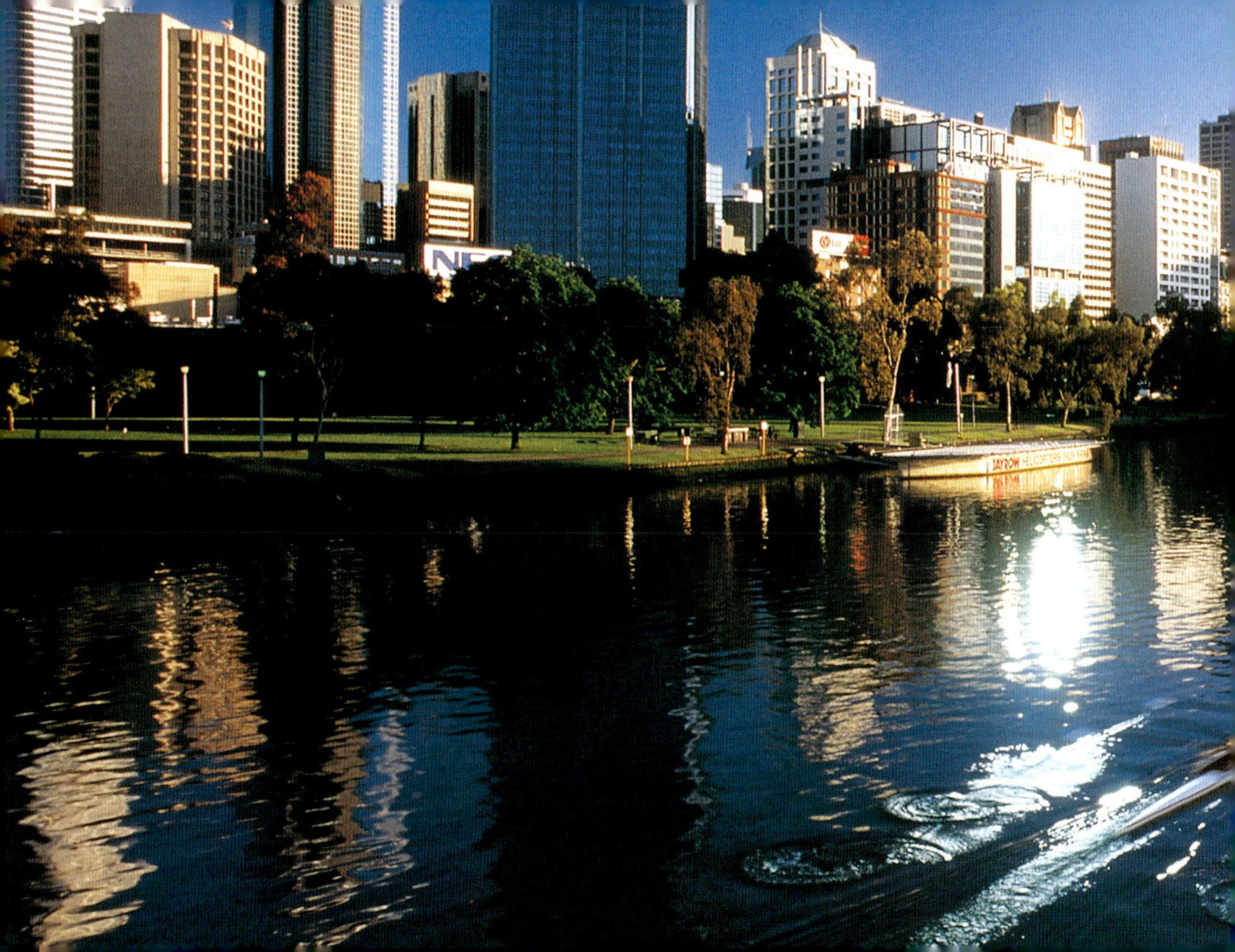
JAYROW

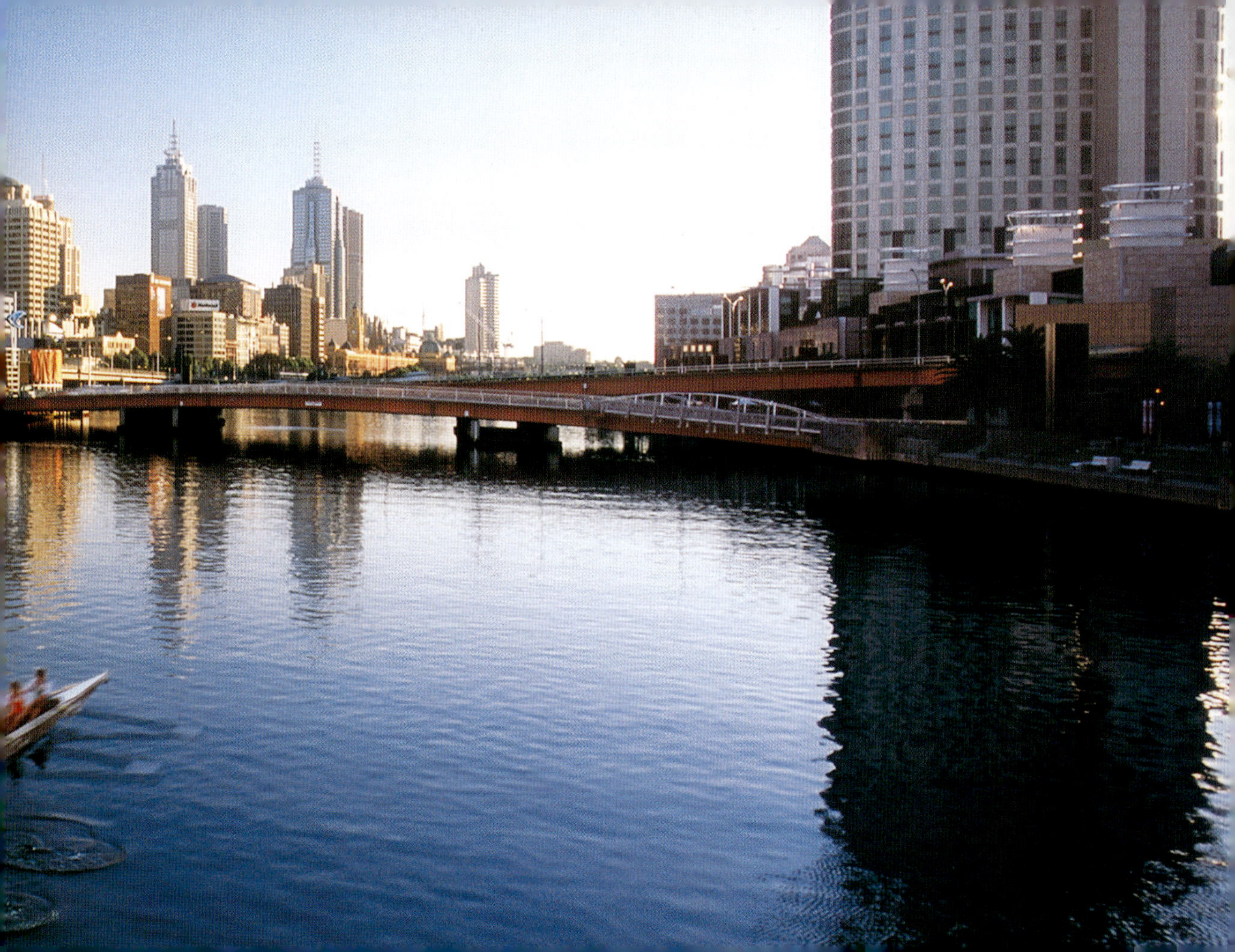

114 Chinatown bustles with activity day and night

CAFE
EzyCom
Sold here
UNIDIAL
FORTUNA VILLAGE
Target Centre
Wilson Parking
SOLD HERE

116 Melbourne's many bars and restaurants make the city come alive at night

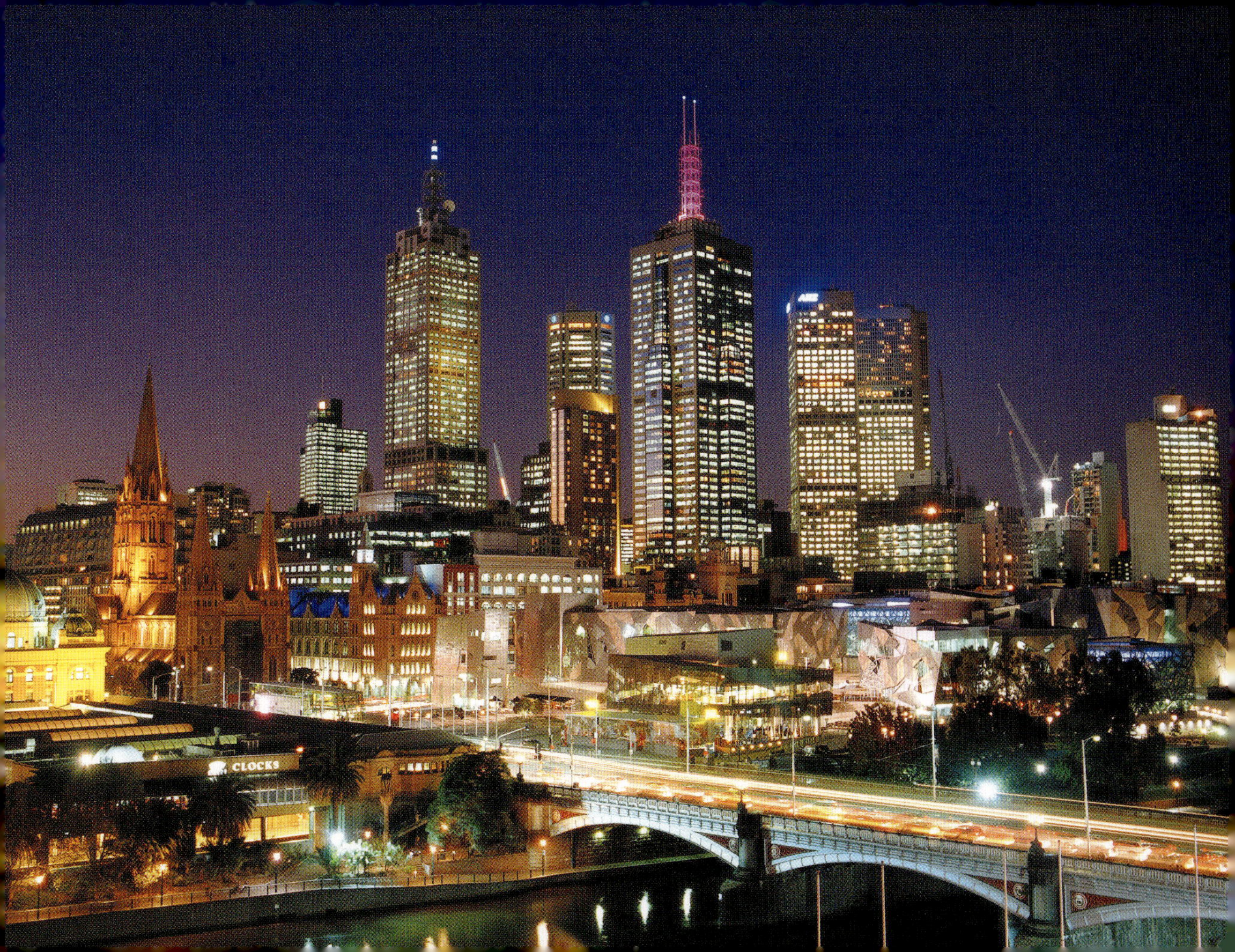
CLOCKS

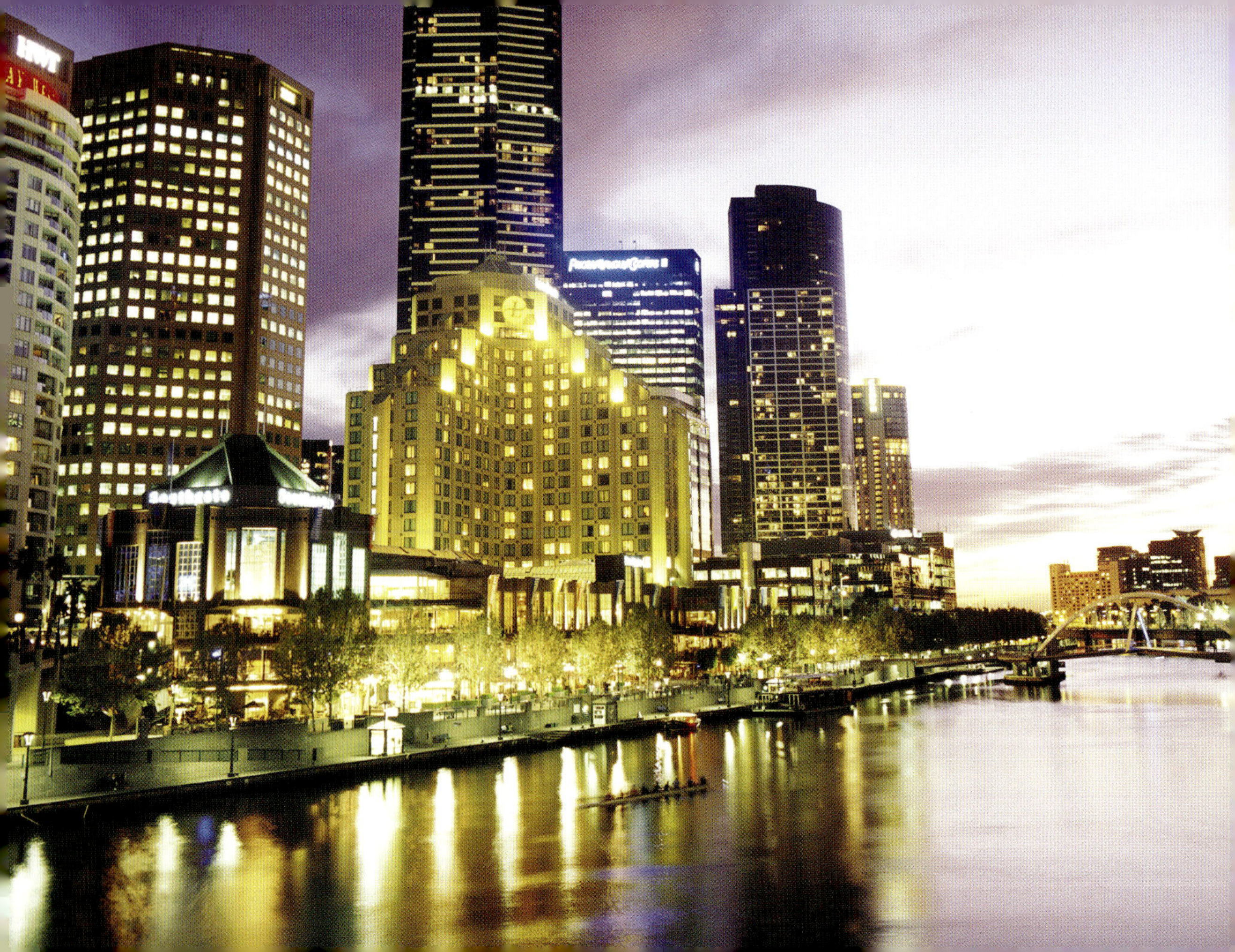
HWT
Southgate

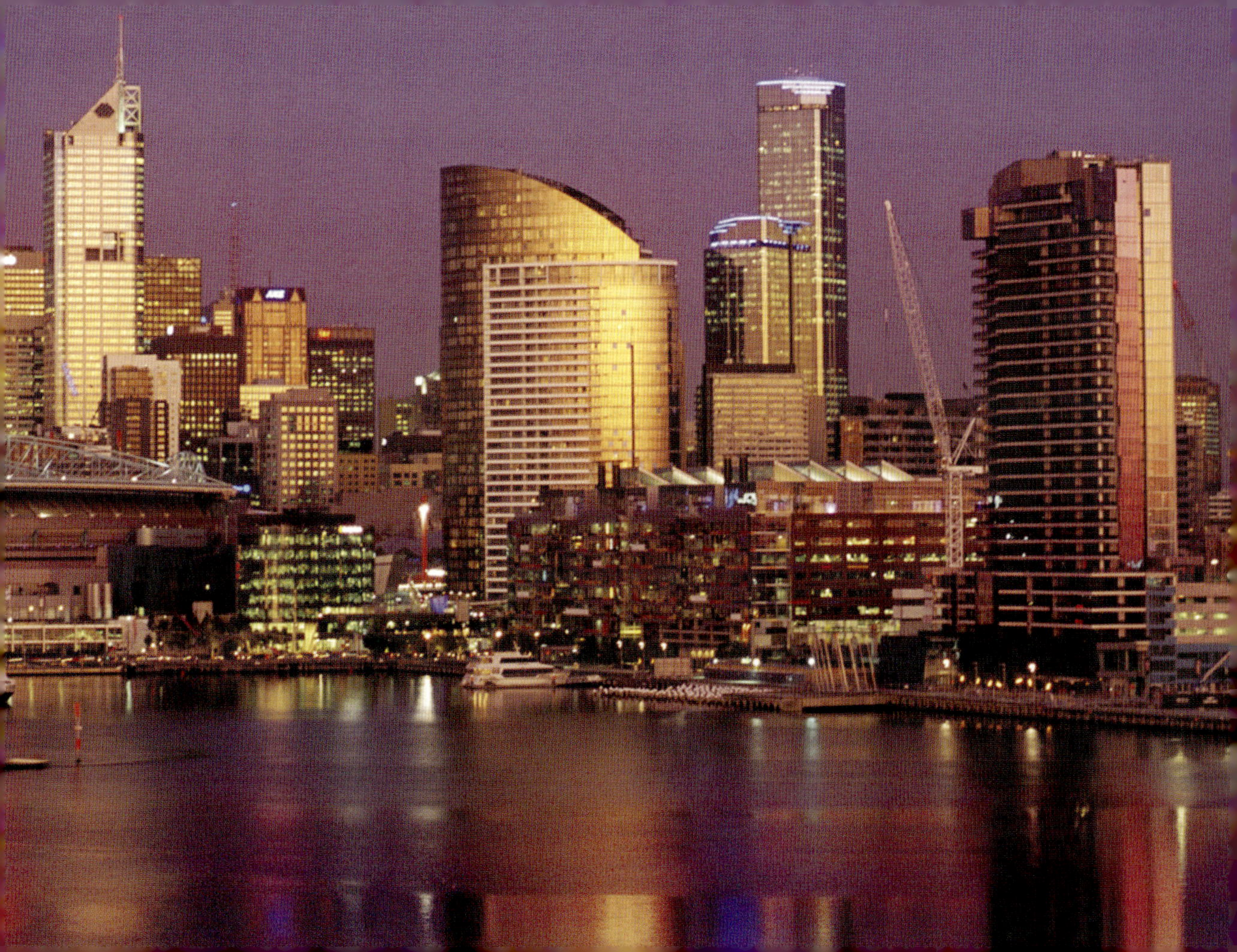

Melbourne is known for its fabulous shopping and cafes

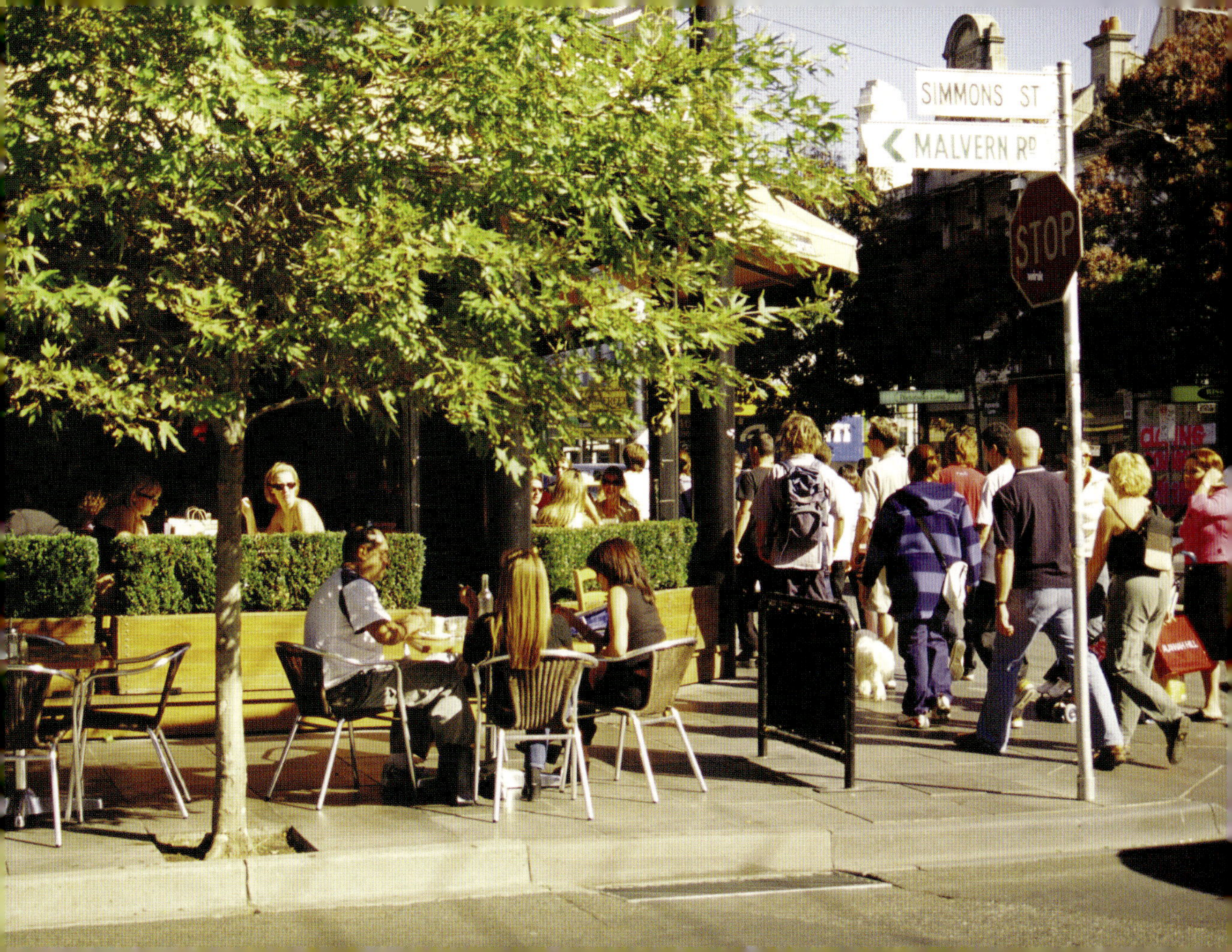
SIMMONS ST
MALVERN RD
STOP

122 The nation stops to watch the Melbourne Cup

Melbourne is host to the Grand Prix *123*

124 A jetty at Lakes Entrance

Westgate Bridge crosses the Yarra River

126 Moon jellyfish at Melbourne Aquarium

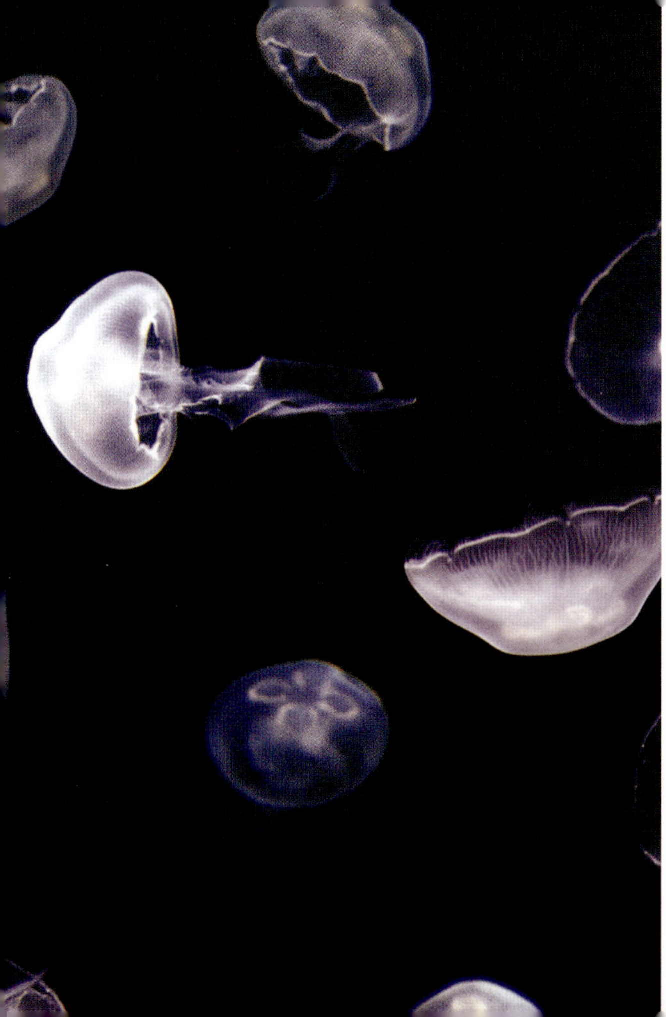
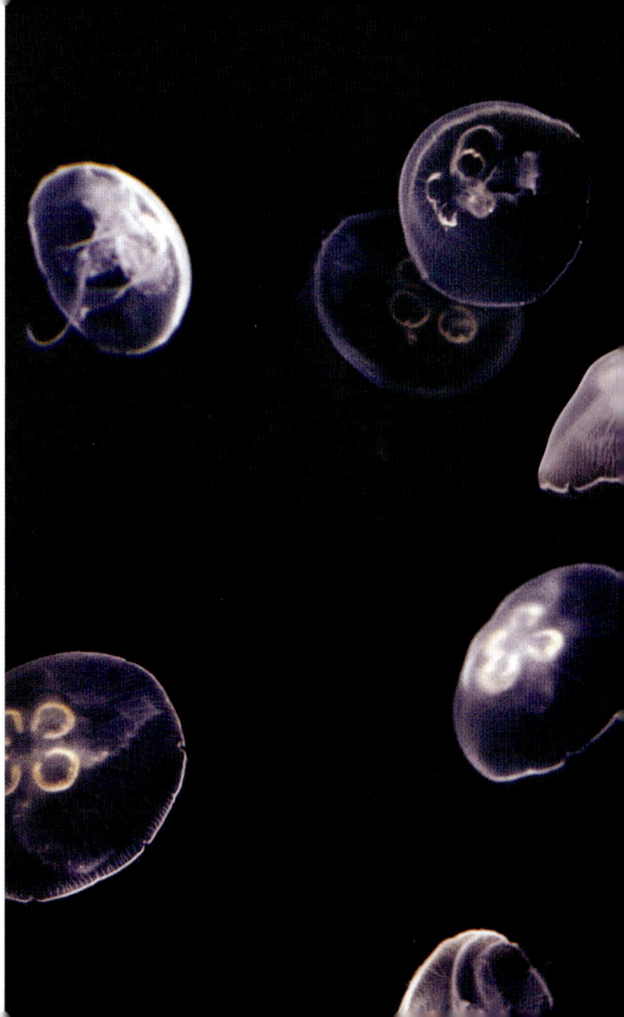

128 The Nobbies on Phillip Island are home to Australia's largest colony of fur seals

Brighton Beach near Melbourne. Next page: Bathing boxes give the beach an old-fashioned feel

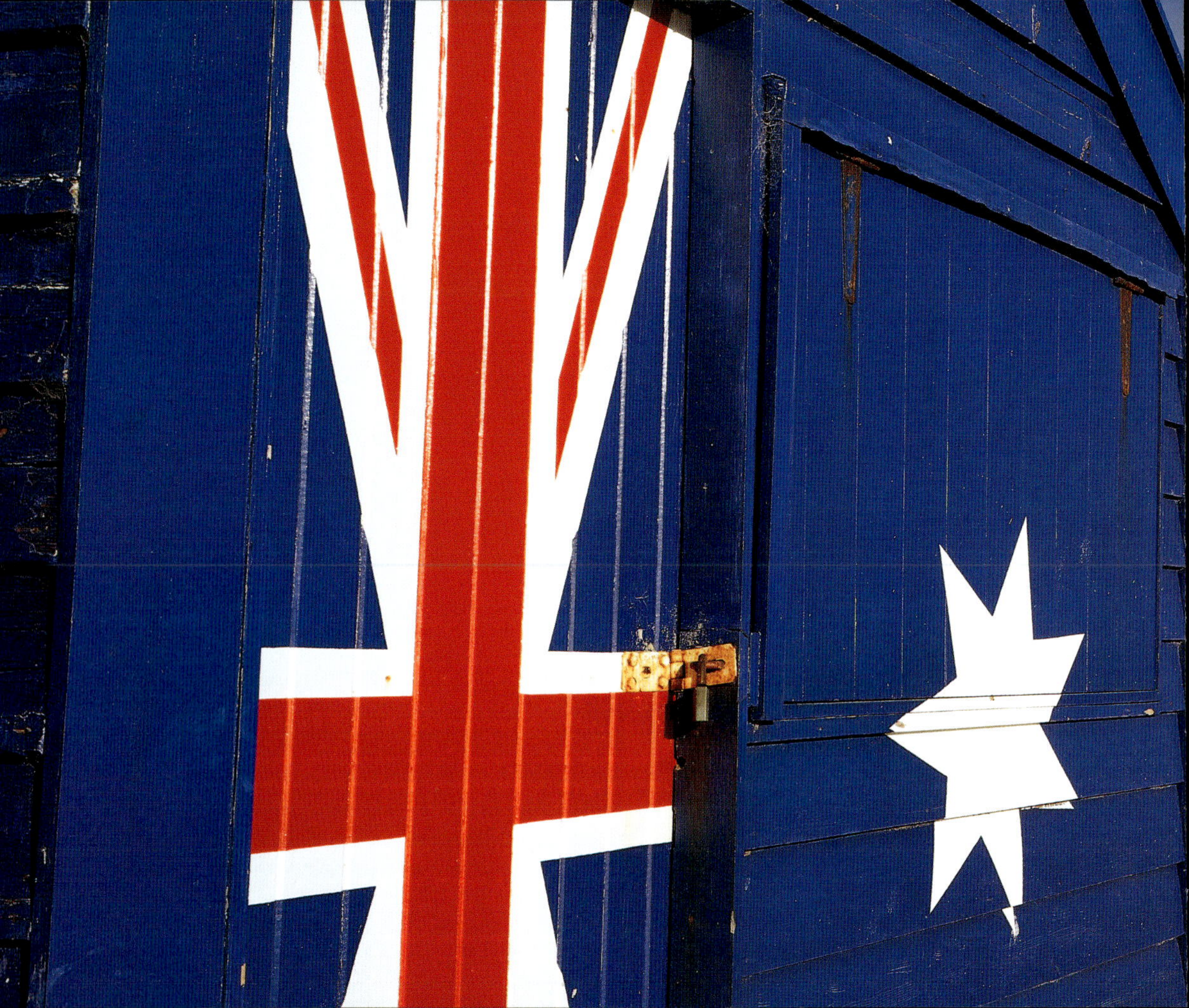

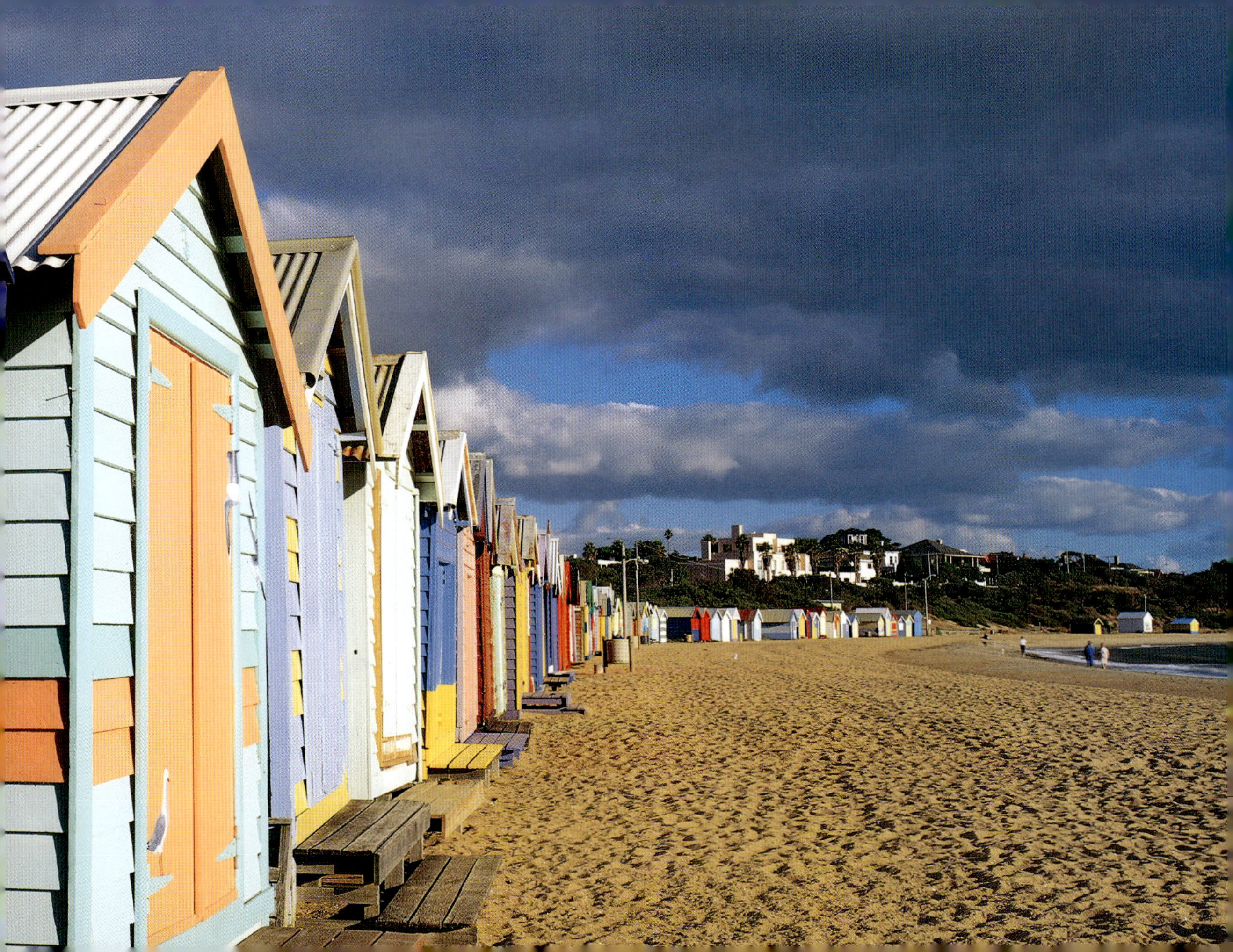

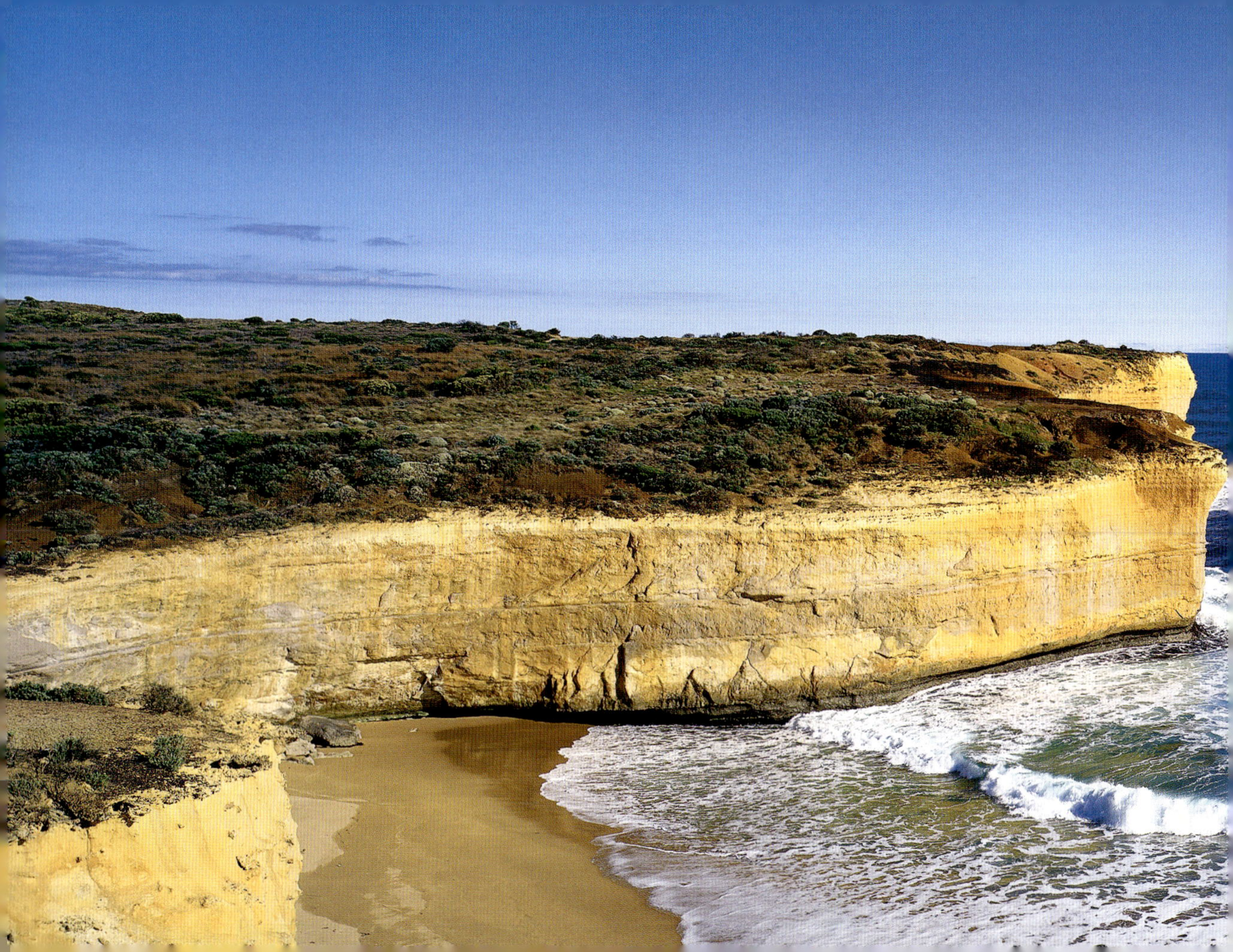

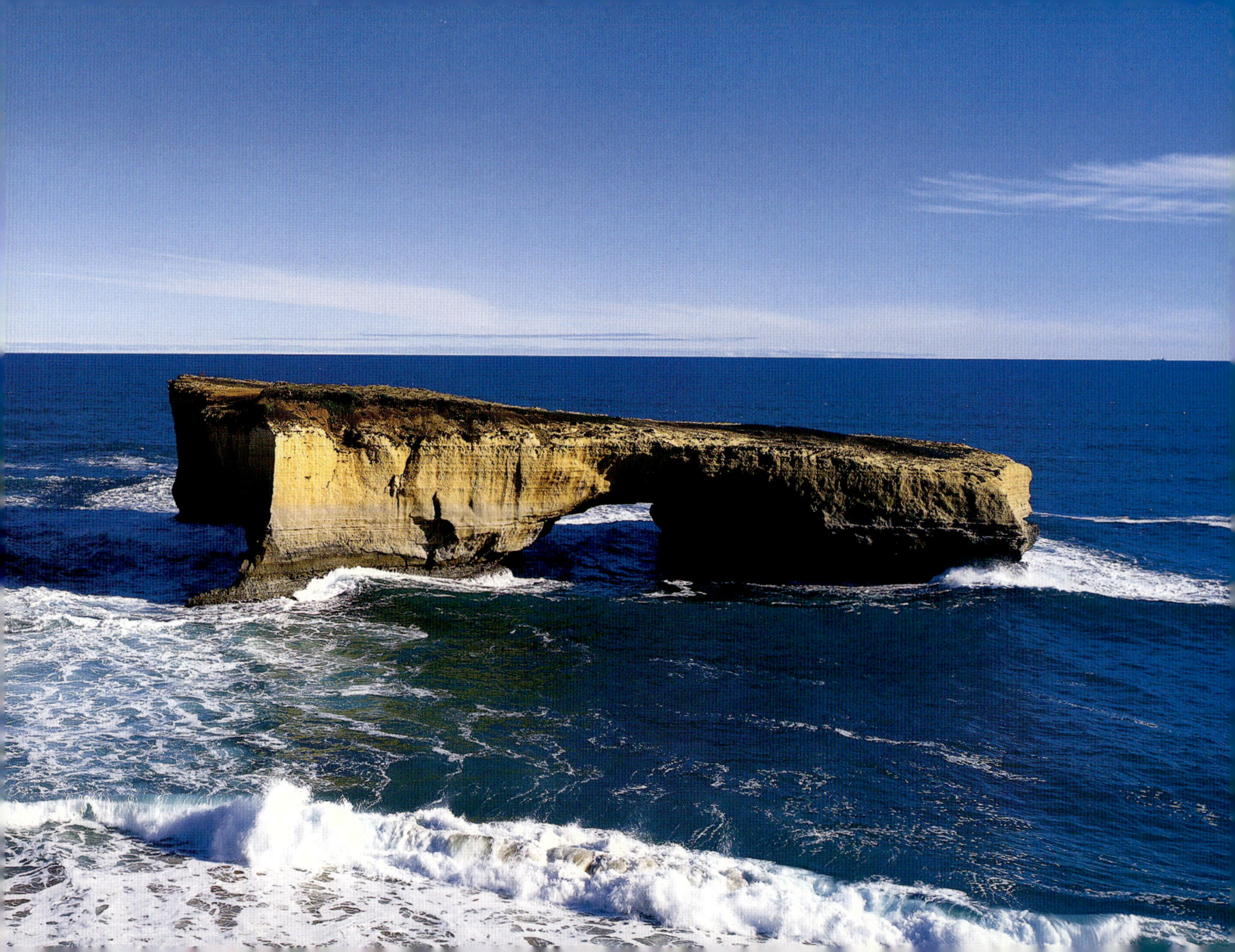

The Twelve Apostles form a collection of limestone stacks nestled together just off the Great Ocean Road.
Next and previous pages: water has eroded some of the area's rock formations

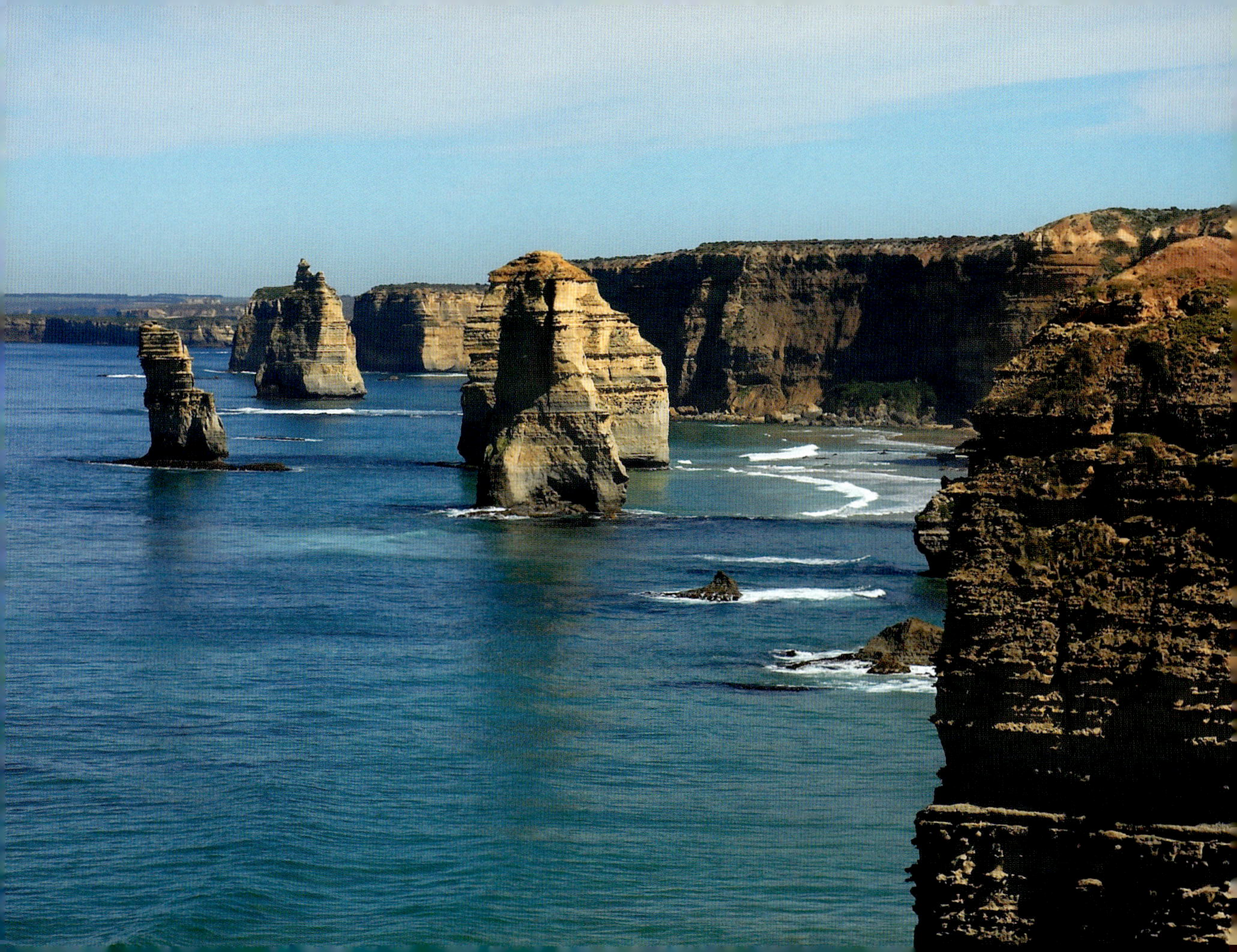

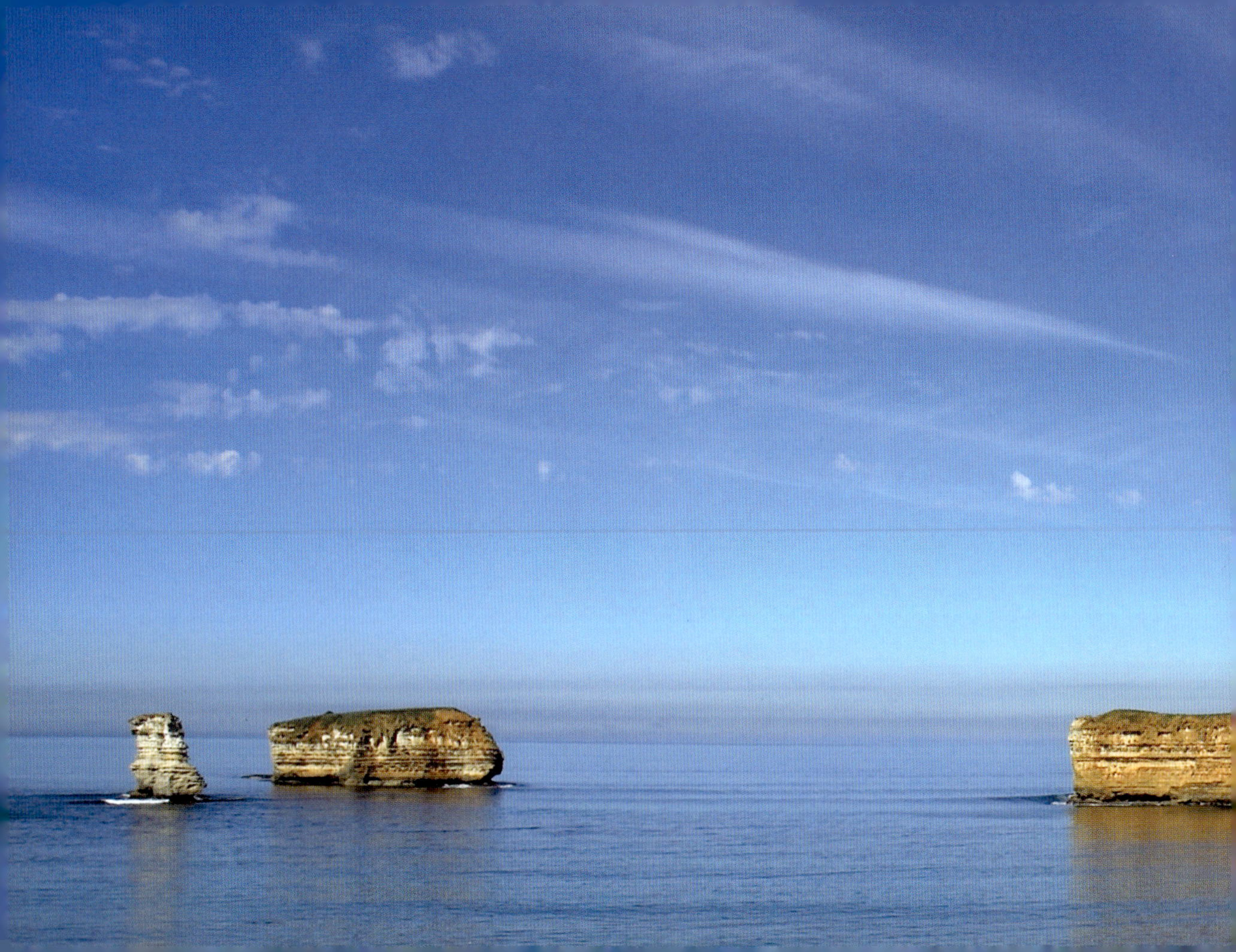

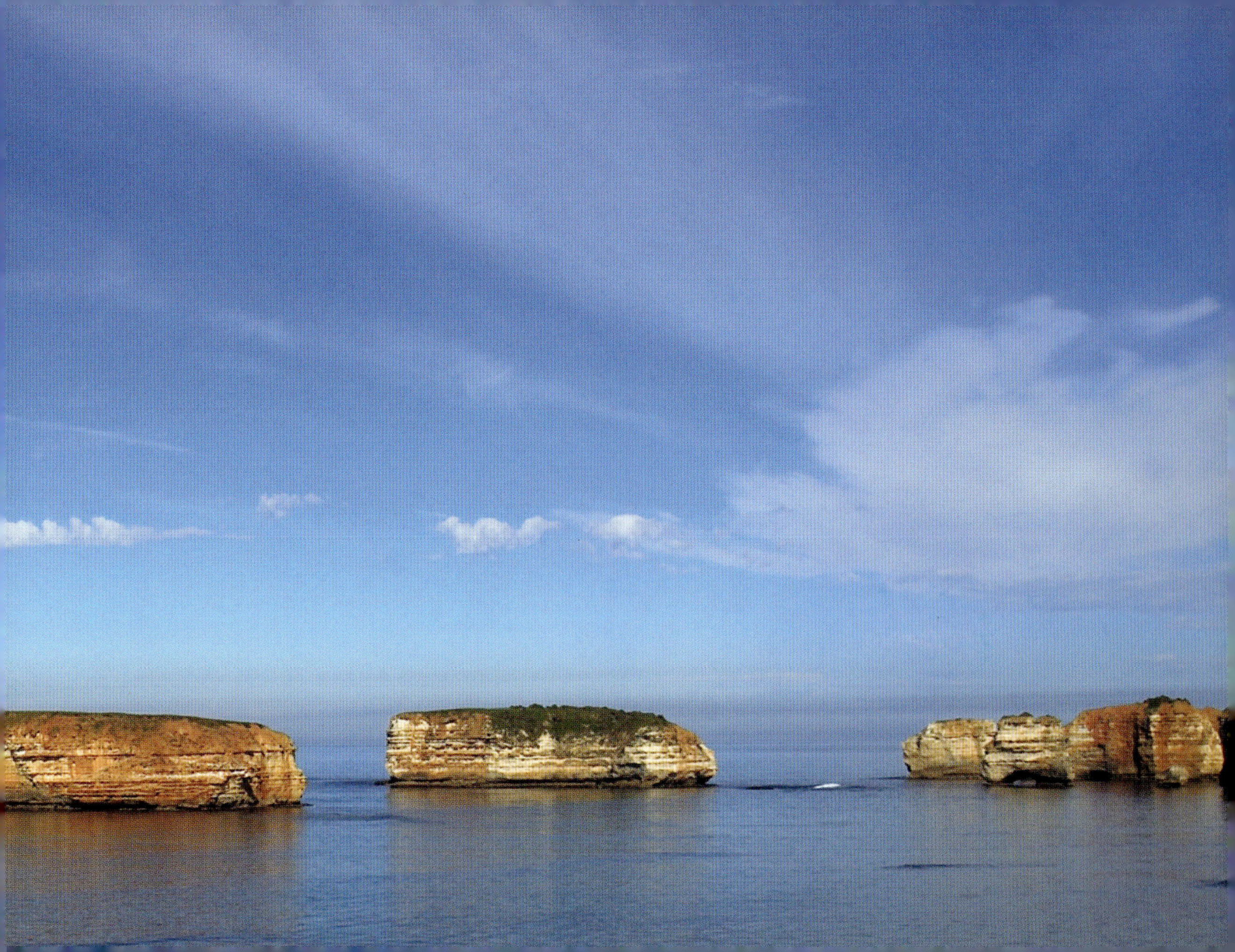

138 Seaford is the gateway to the Mornington Peninsula

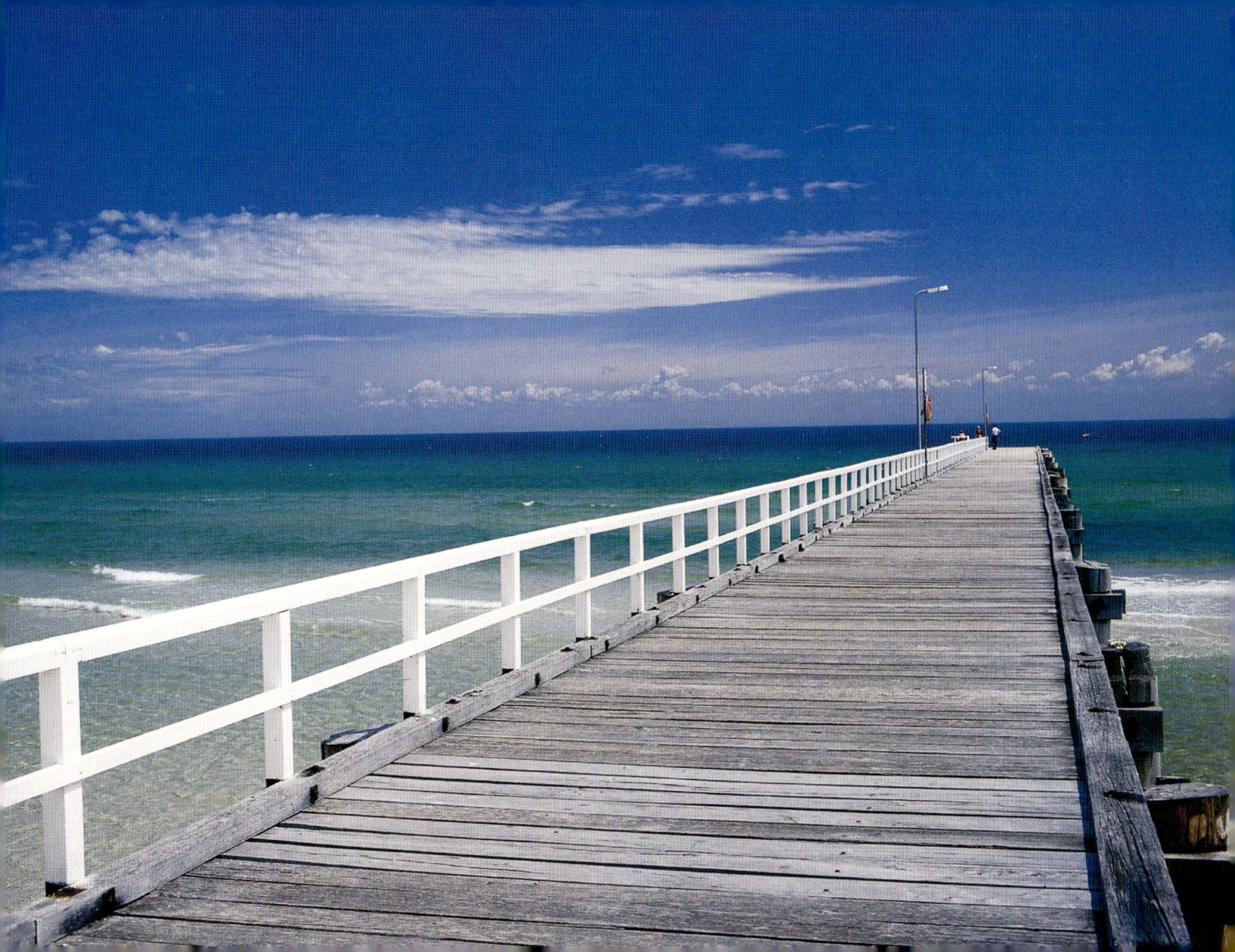

140 The Ozone Hotel at Queenscliff

Castlemaine in central Victoria was originally a thriving gold mining town – 141

142 A houseboat on the Murray River near Echuca

Gunbower Island lies on the Murray River. Next page: Maroondah Highway in the Black Spur Forest 143

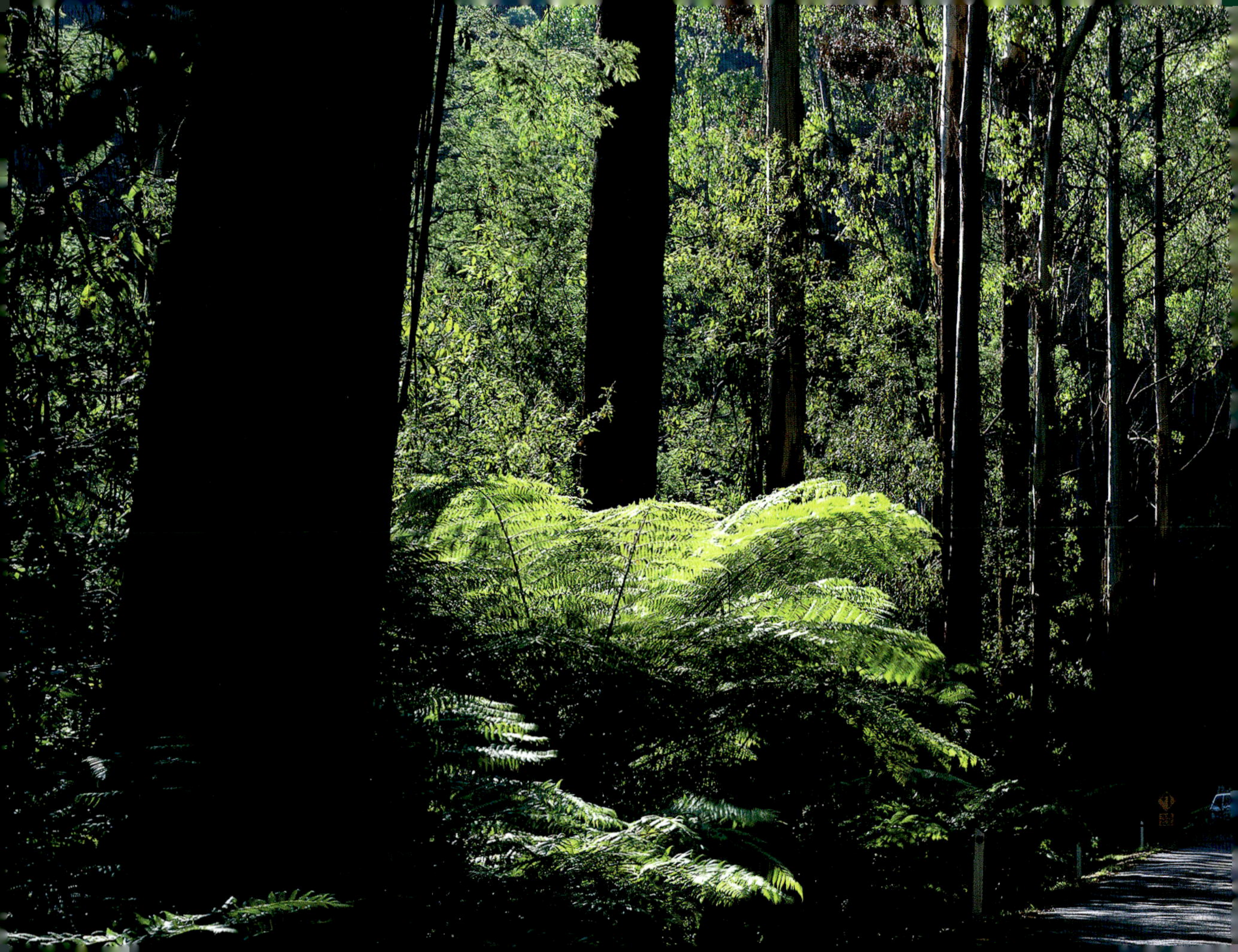

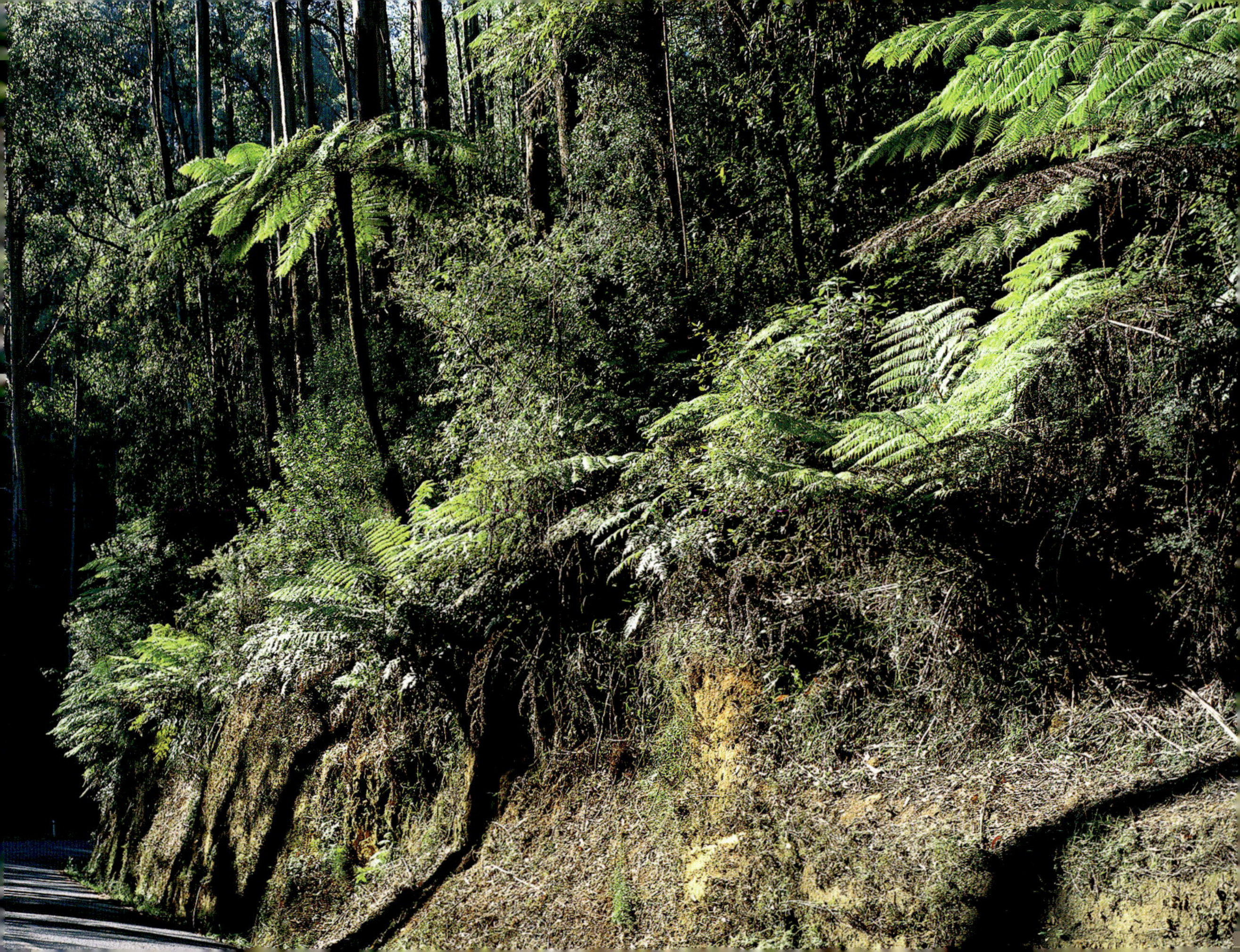

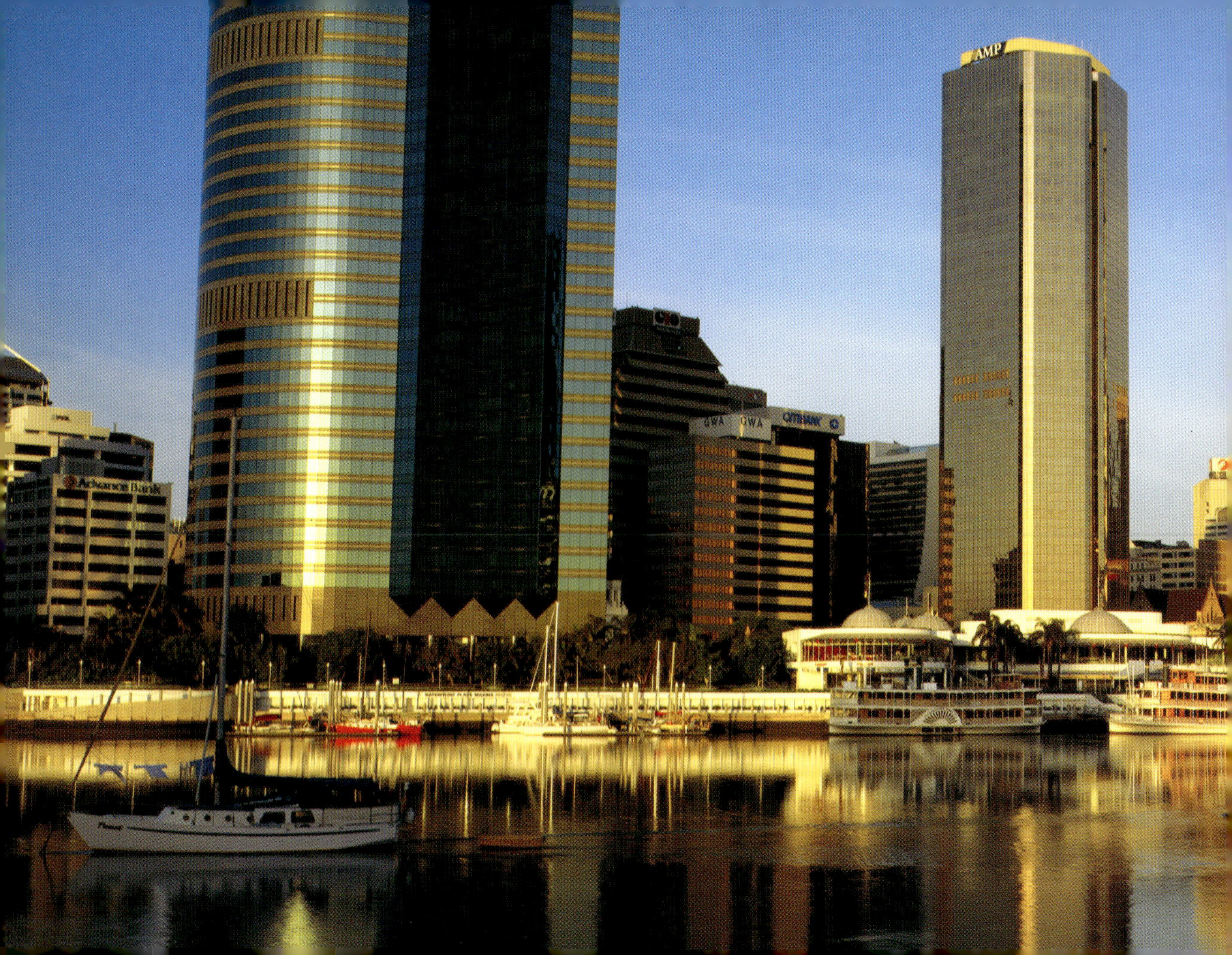
AMP
Advance Bank
GWA
GWA

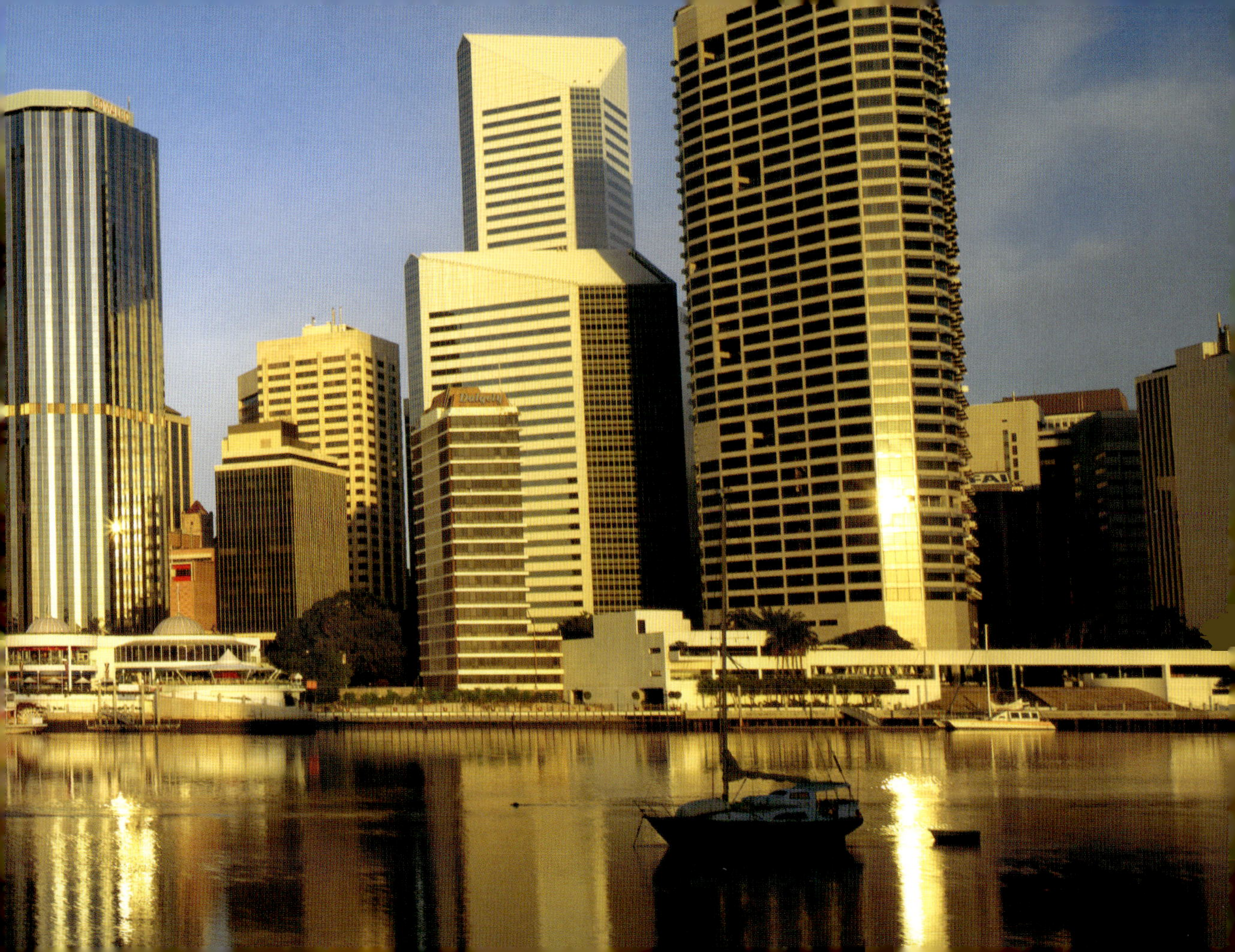
FAI

148 The Brisbane River flows through the city of Brisbane before emptying into Moreton Bay

Katherine Gorge in Nitmiluk National Park is a great spot for canoeing   247

This edition published in 2013 by New Holland Publishers Pty Ltd
London • Sydney • Cape Town • Auckland

Garfield House 86–88 Edgware Road London W2 2EA United Kingdom
1/66 Gibbes Street Chatswood NSW 2067 Australia
Wembley Square First Floor Solan Road Gardens Cape Town 8001 South Africa
218 Lake Road Northcote Auckland New Zealand

www.newhollandpublishers.com

Copyright © 2013 New Holland Publishers Pty Ltd

All images New Holland Image Library and Graeme Gillies except as below:
Copyright in pictures: p122 Roving Eye; pp5, 29, 39, 42, 46–7, 49–51, 52, 54–5, 57, 62–3, 64–7, 70, 72, 74, 75–6, 78–84, 86–88, 90–3 Tourism NSW; pp104–8, 110–2, 114–7, 119–21, 141–2 Tourism Victoria; 236–7, 247 Tourism Northern Territory.

First published in 2008

All rights reserved. No part of this publication may be reproduced, stored in a retrieval system or transmitted, in any form or by any means, electronic, mechanical, photocopying, recording or otherwise, without the prior written permission of the publishers and copyright holders.

A record of this book is held at the National Library of Australia.

ISBN 9781742574097

Managing Director: Fiona Schultz
Cover Designer: Kimberley Pearce
Production Director: Olga Dementiev
Printer: Toppan Leefung Printing Ltd (China)

10 9 8 7 6 5 4 3 2 1

Keep up with New Holland Publishers on Facebook
www.facebook.com/NewHollandPublishers